NOTEBOOK NO.

Continued From Notebook No.   Continu

ASSIGNED TO:

Name   Date

Date Issued   Signature

Phone   By

Company   Email

Department

Address

City   State   Zip

Date Notebook Complete   Number Of Pages Filled In

Notes:

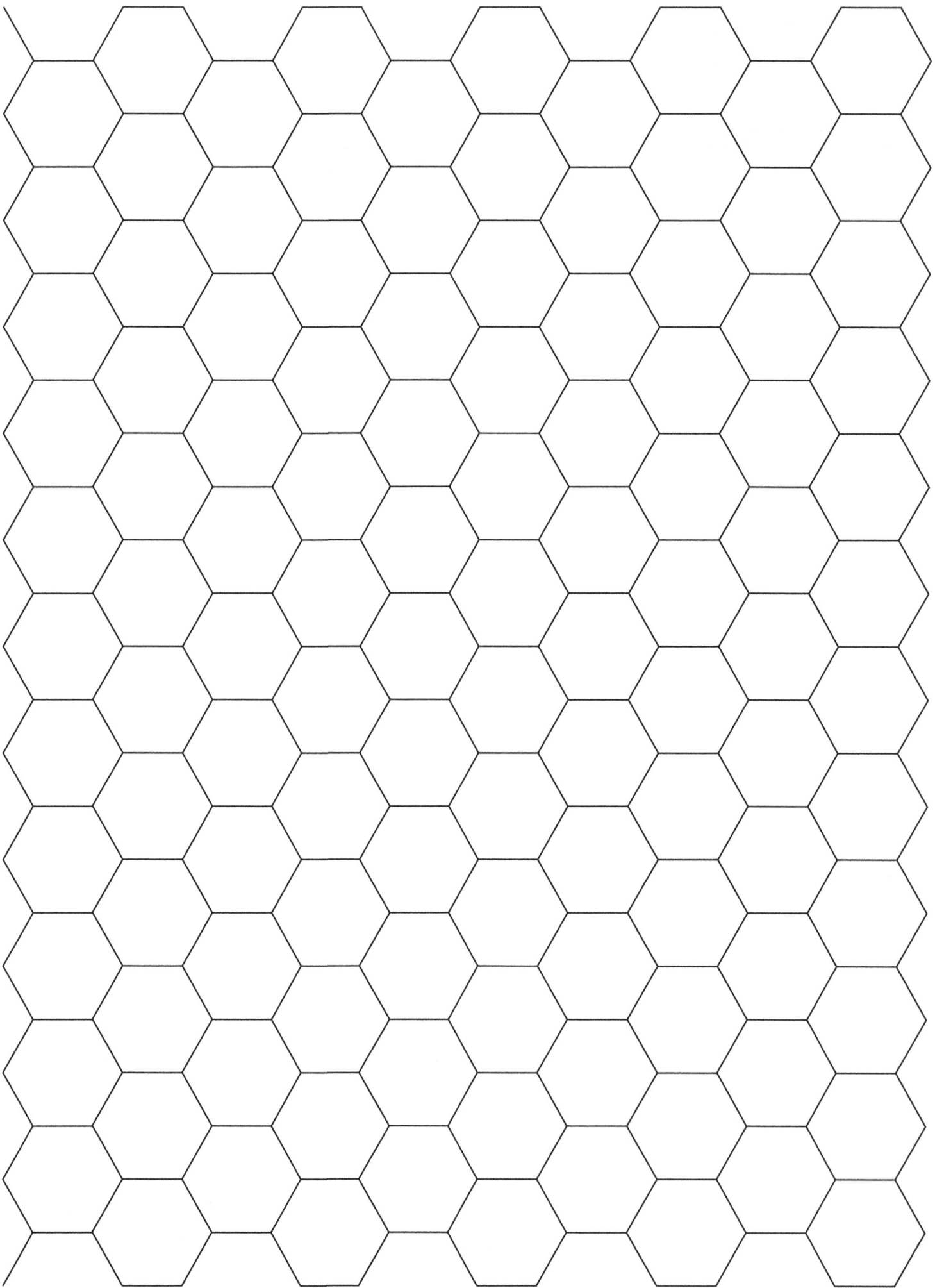

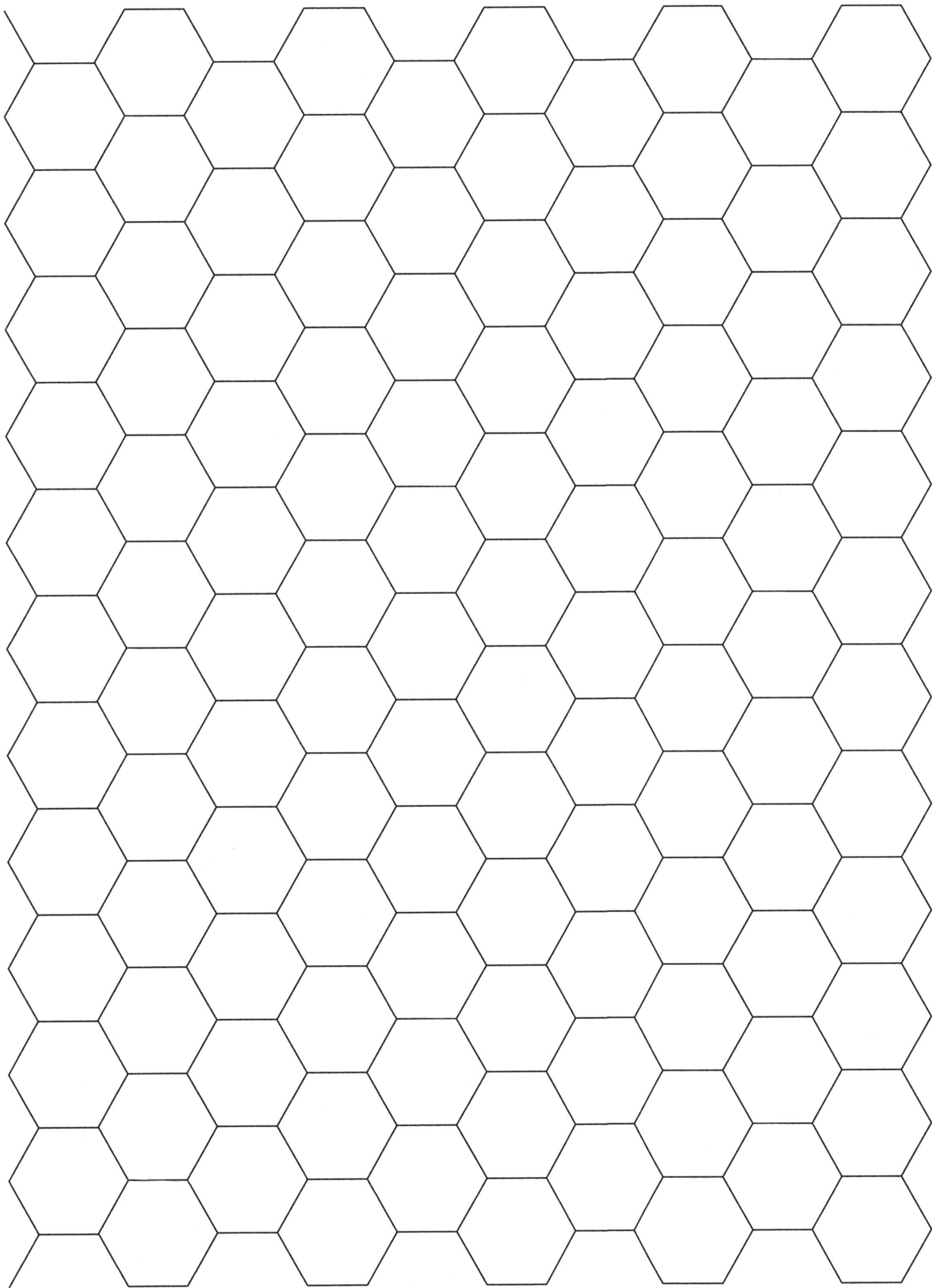

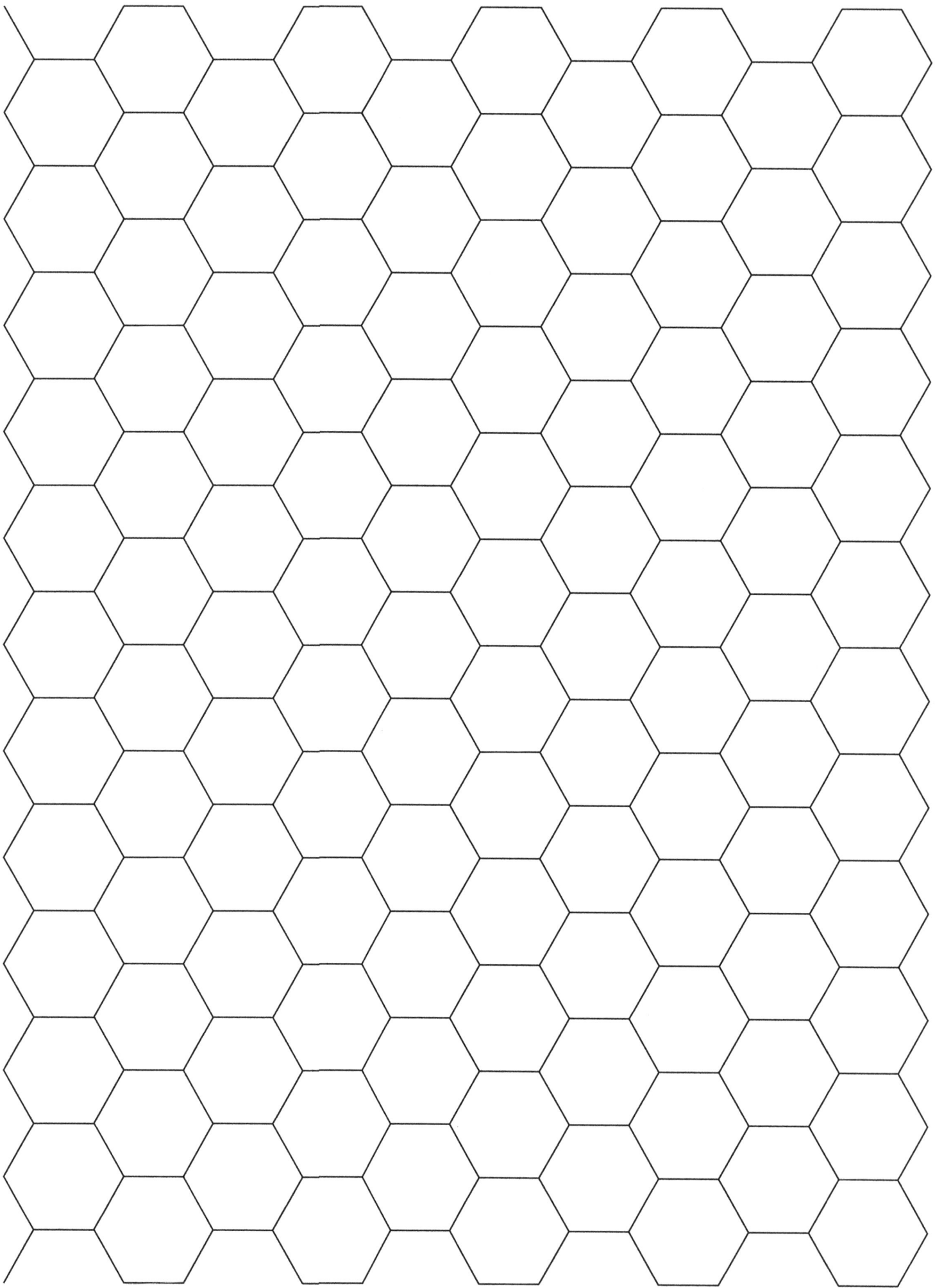

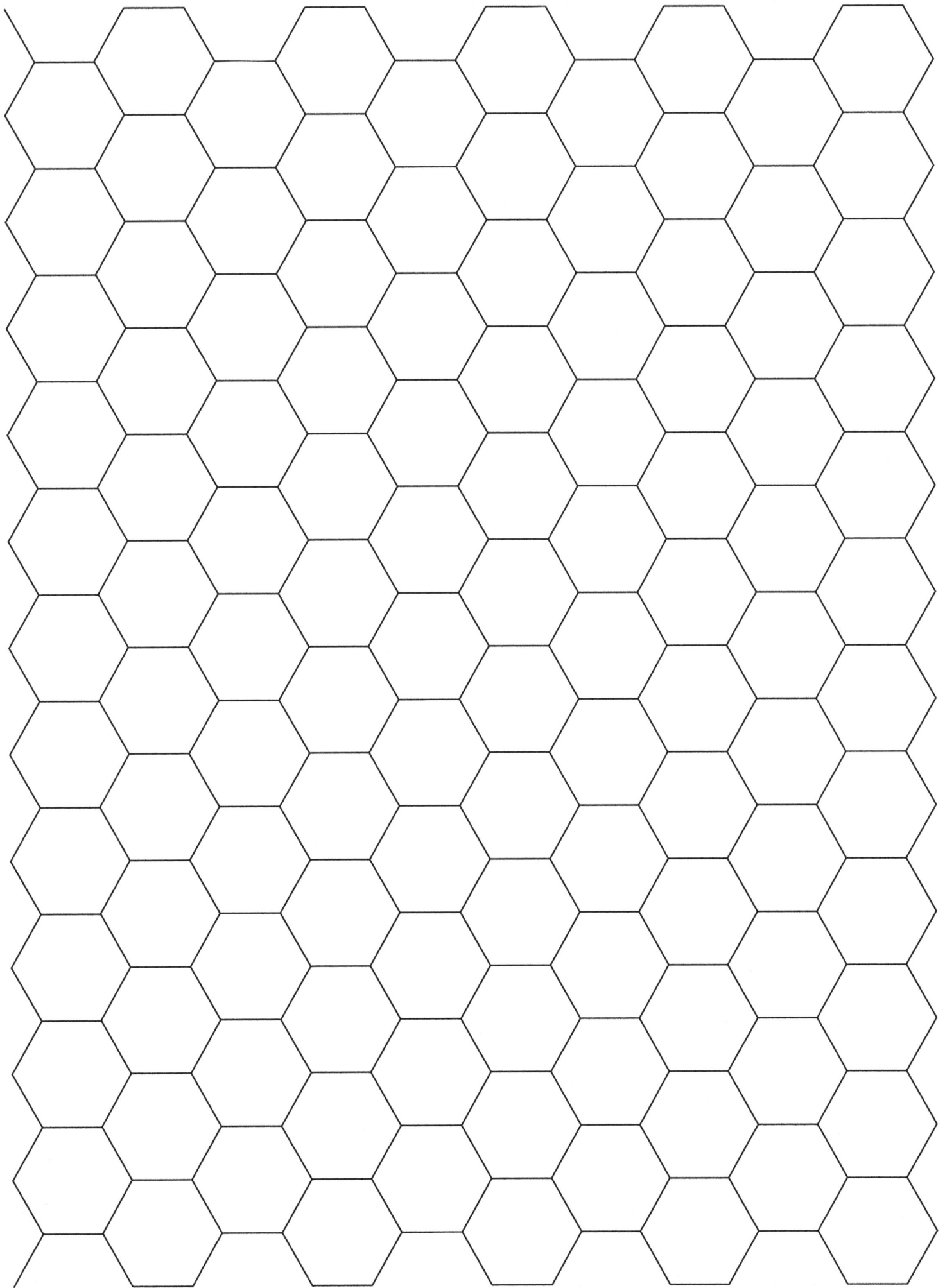

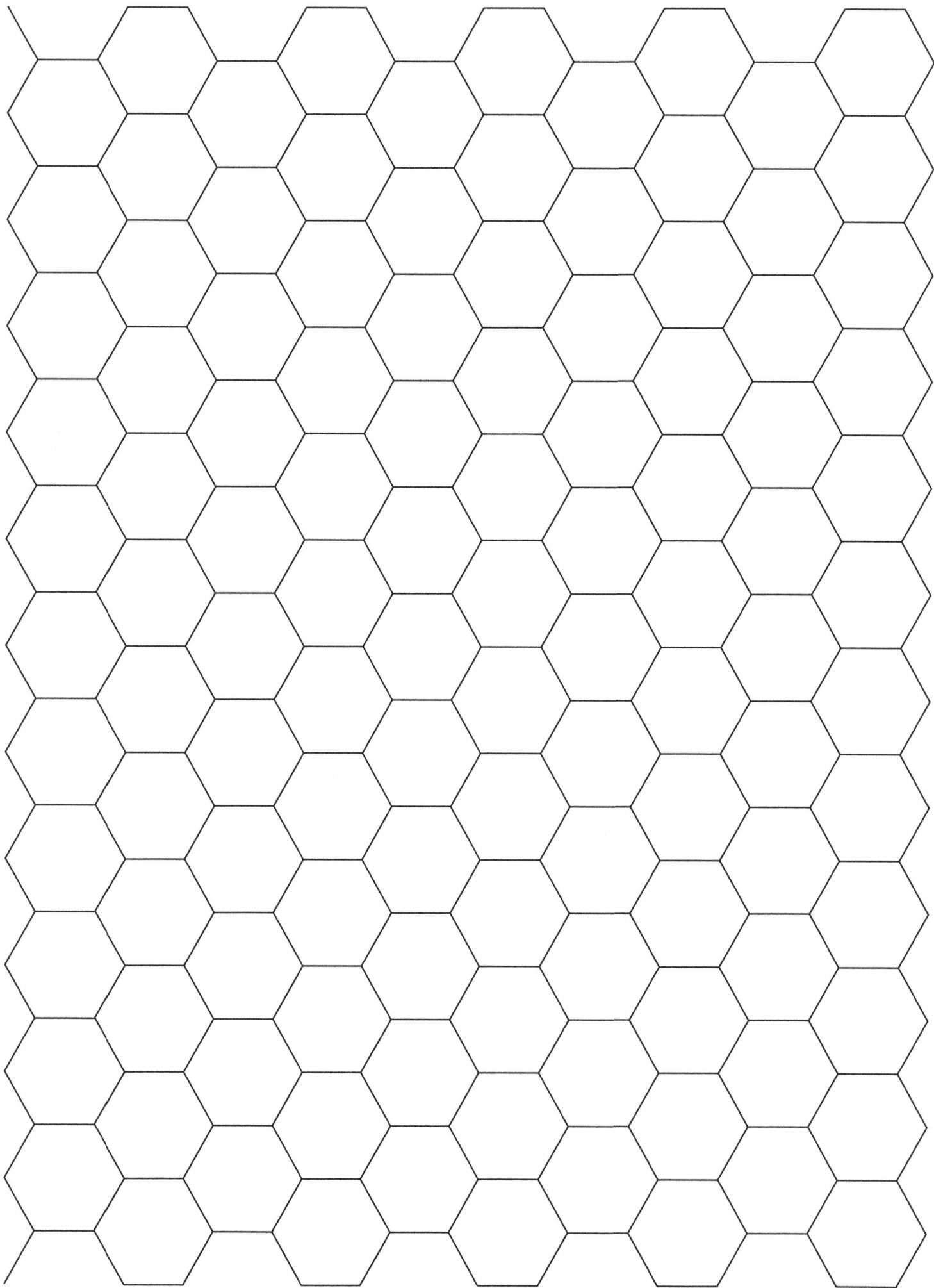

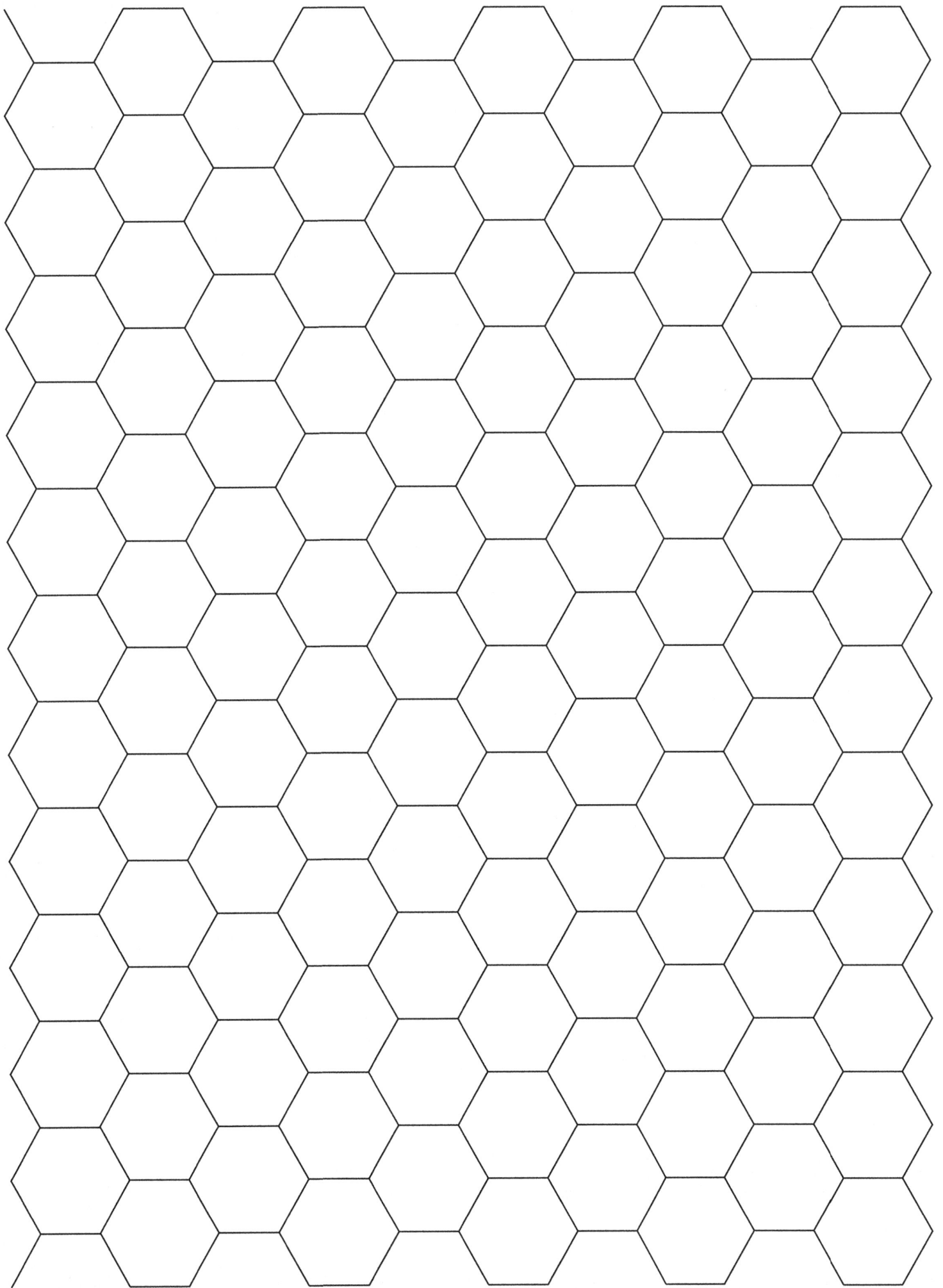

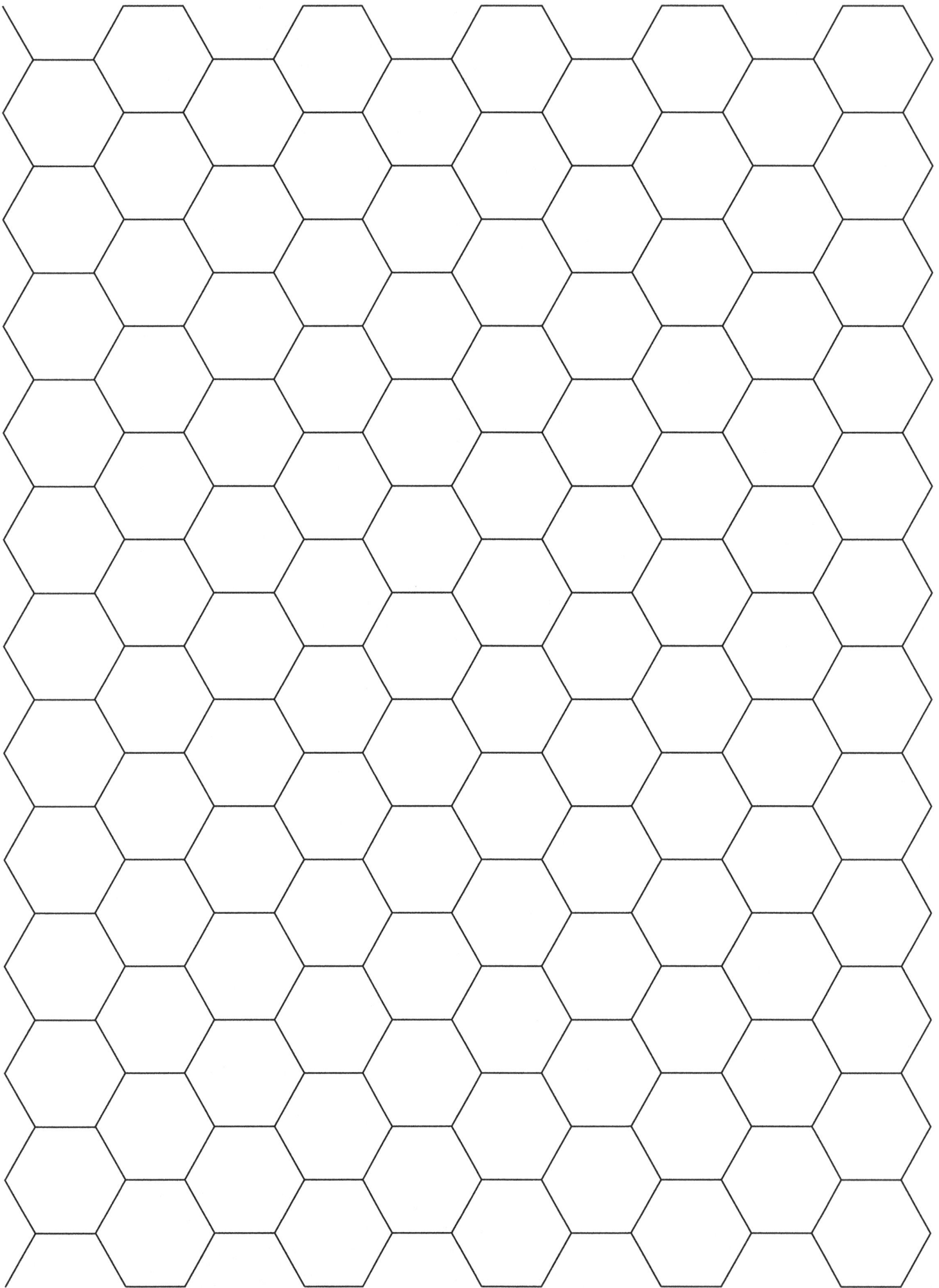

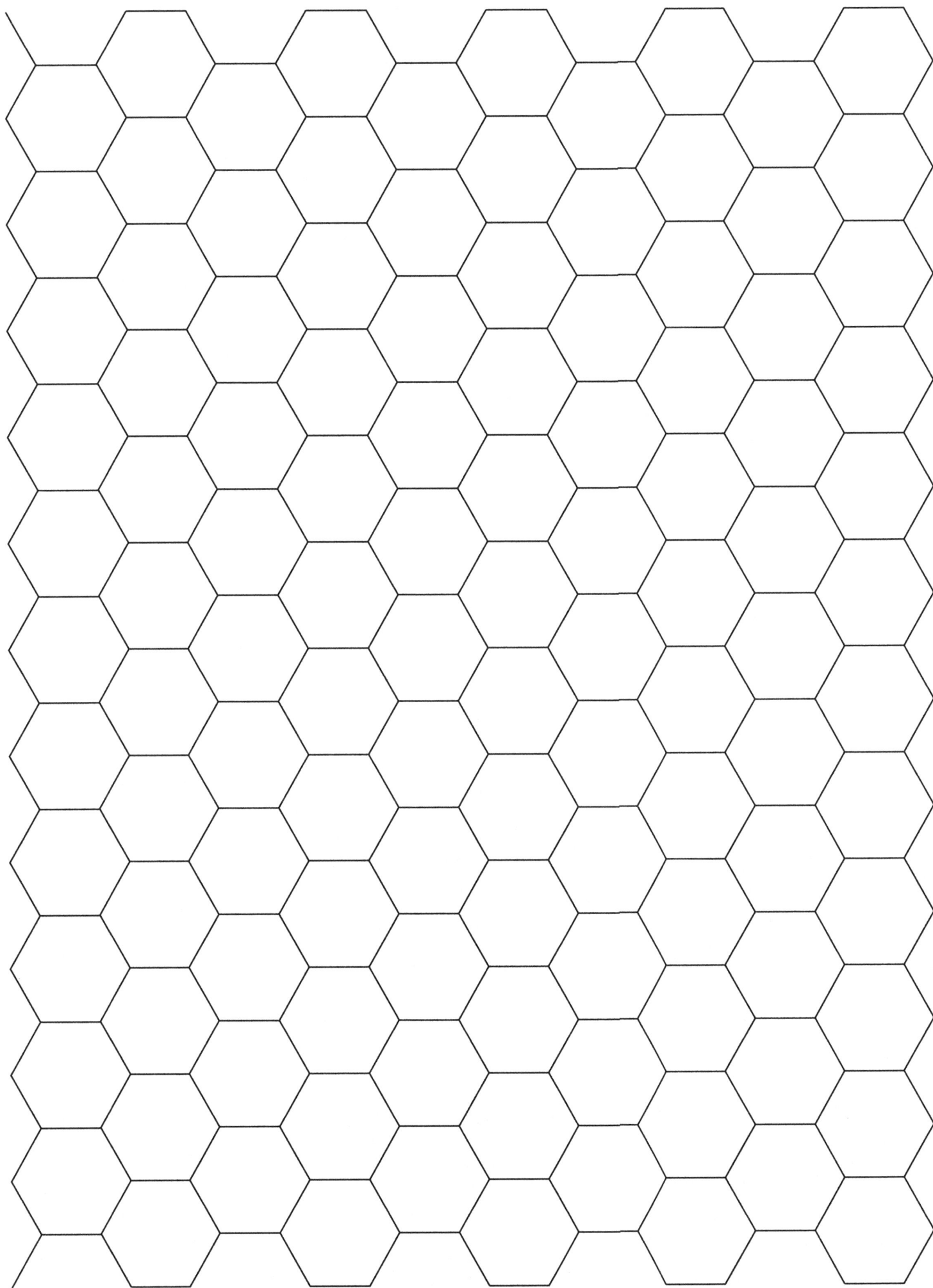

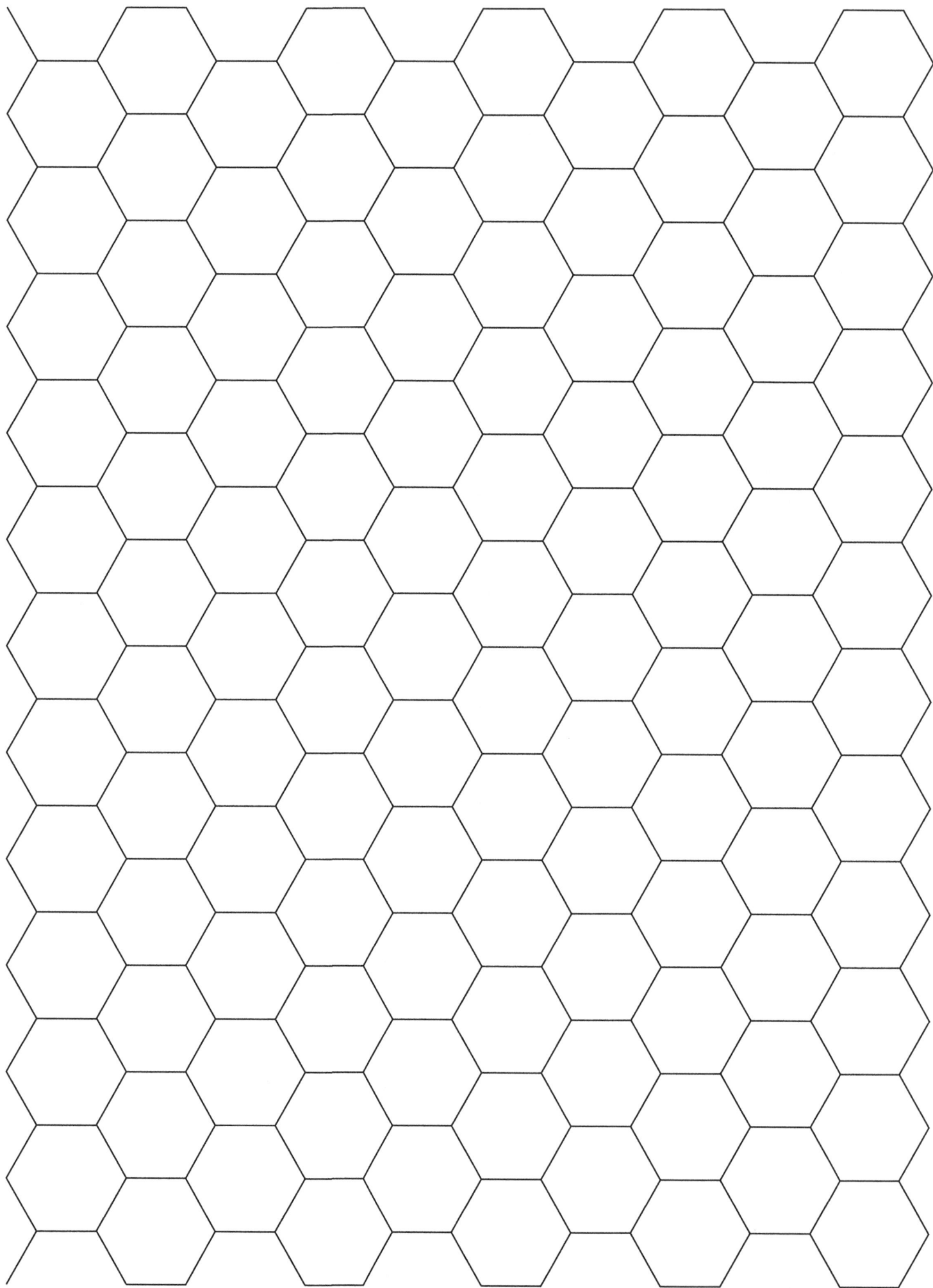

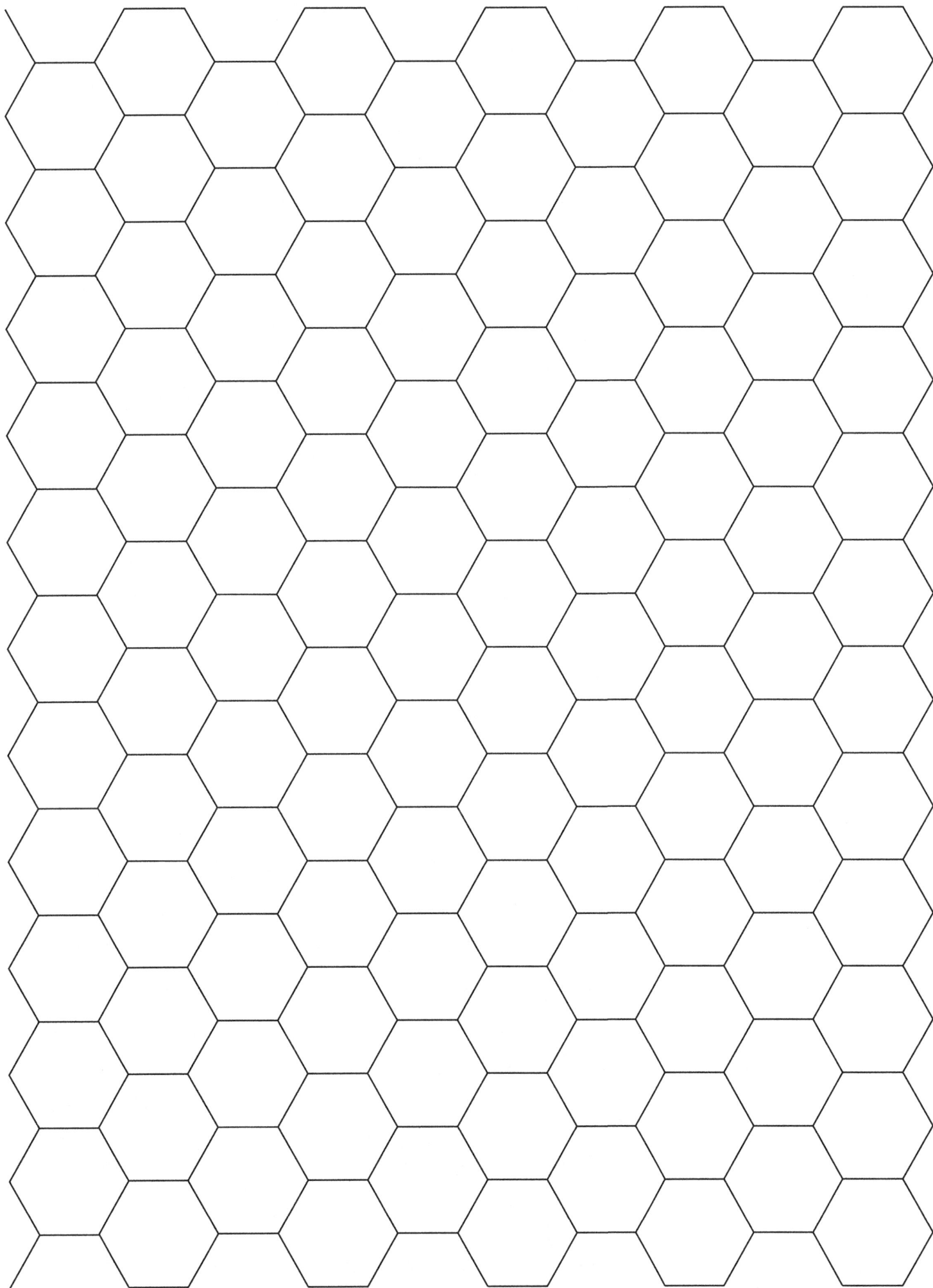

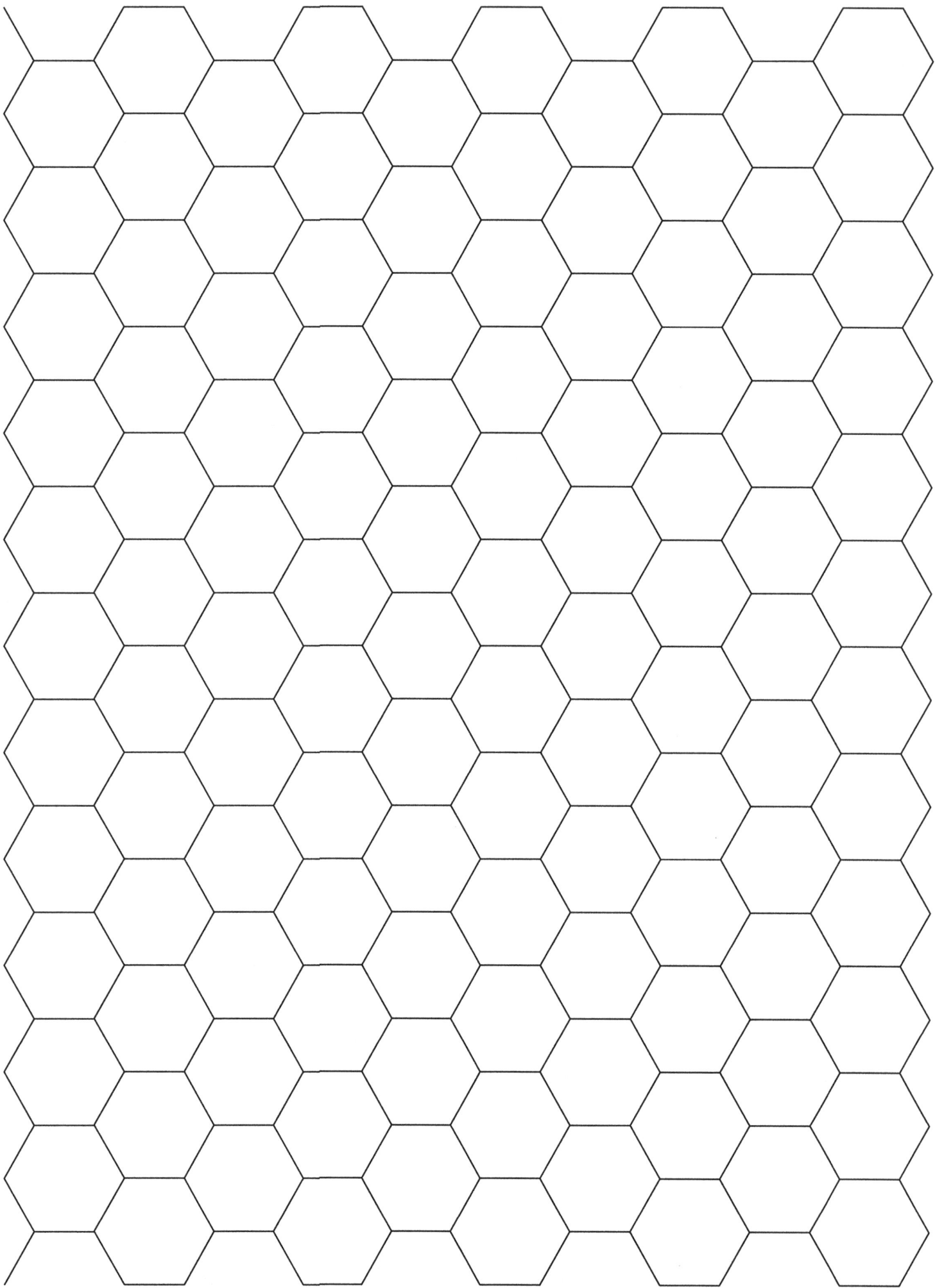

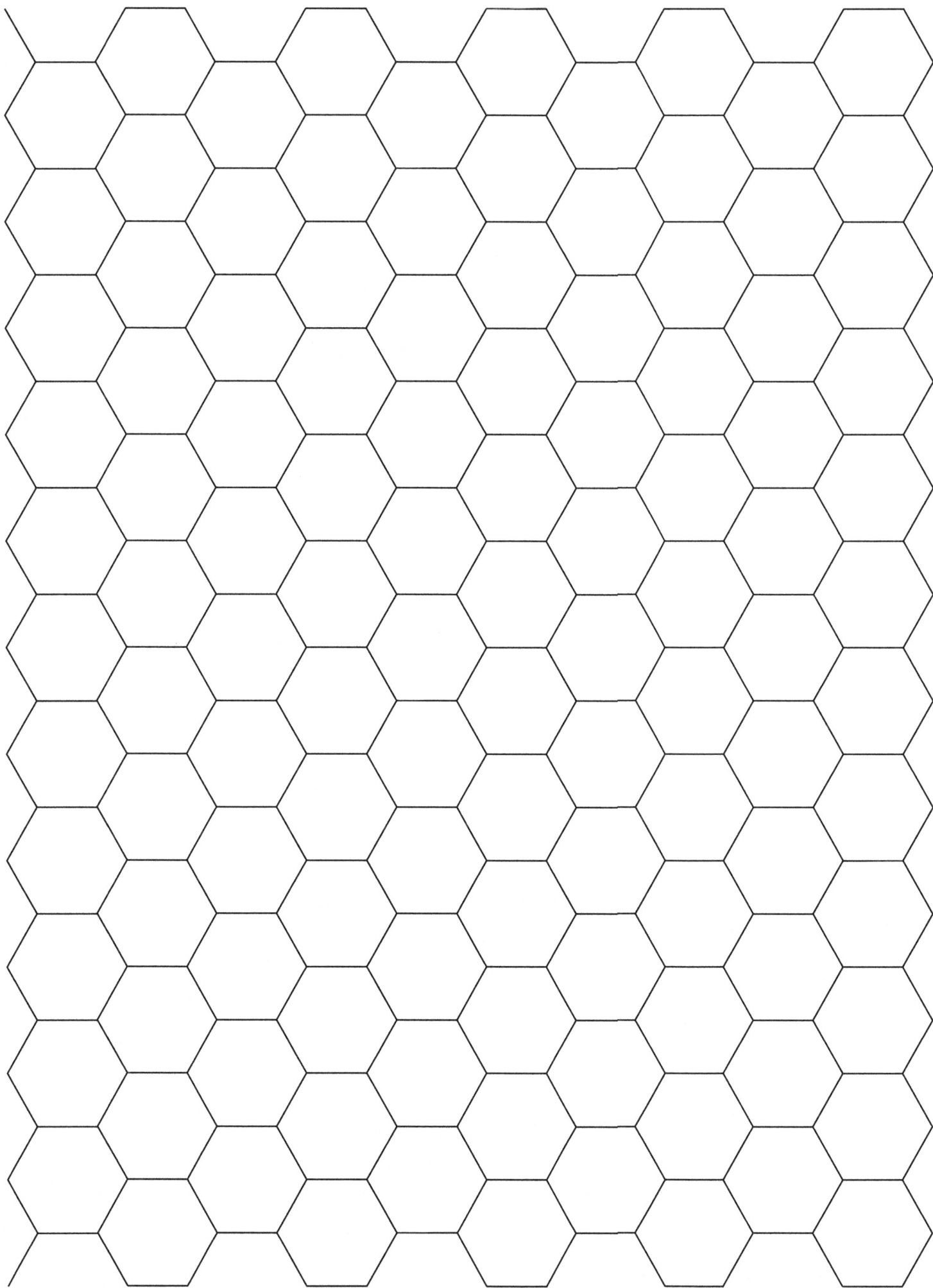

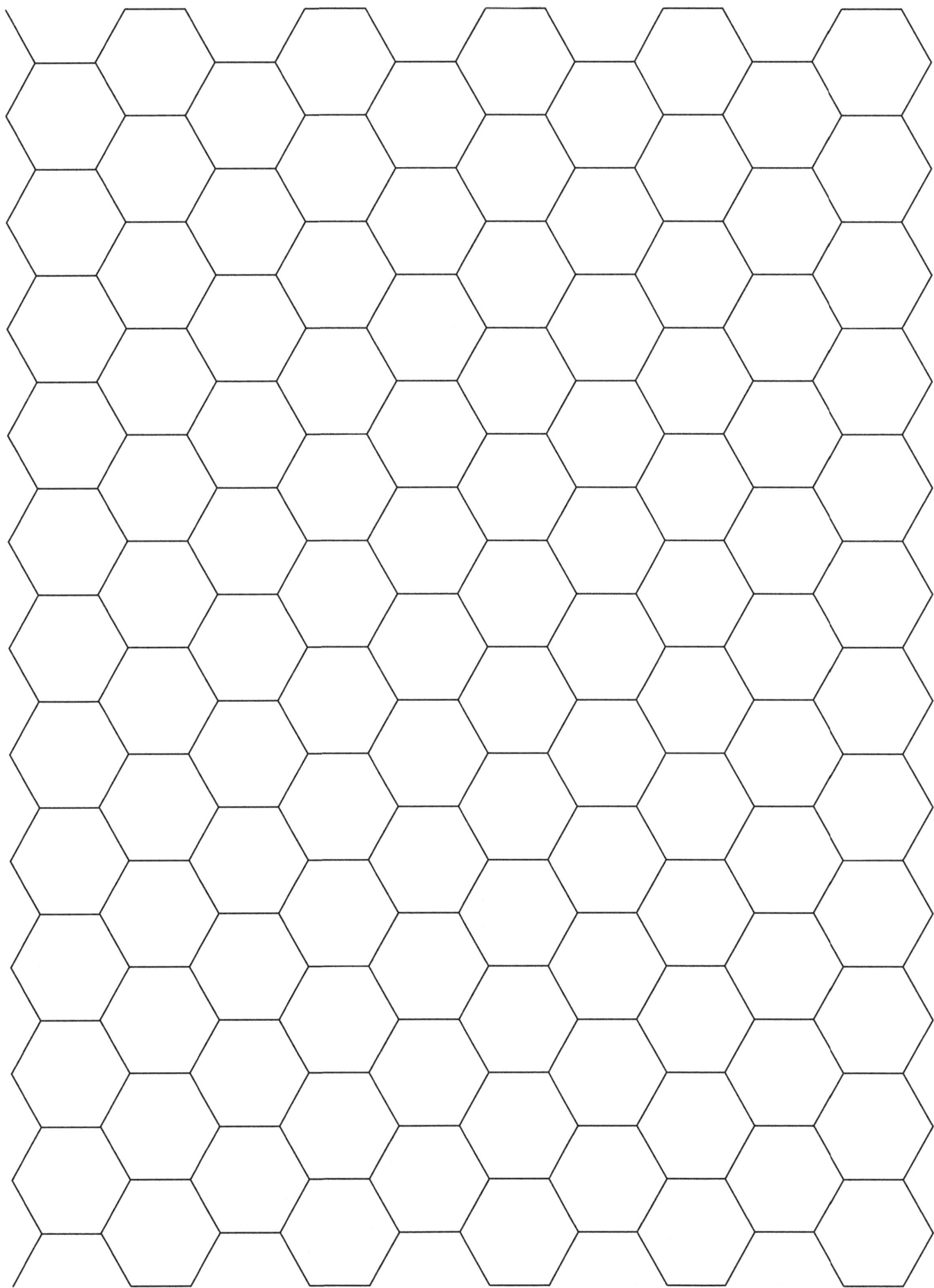

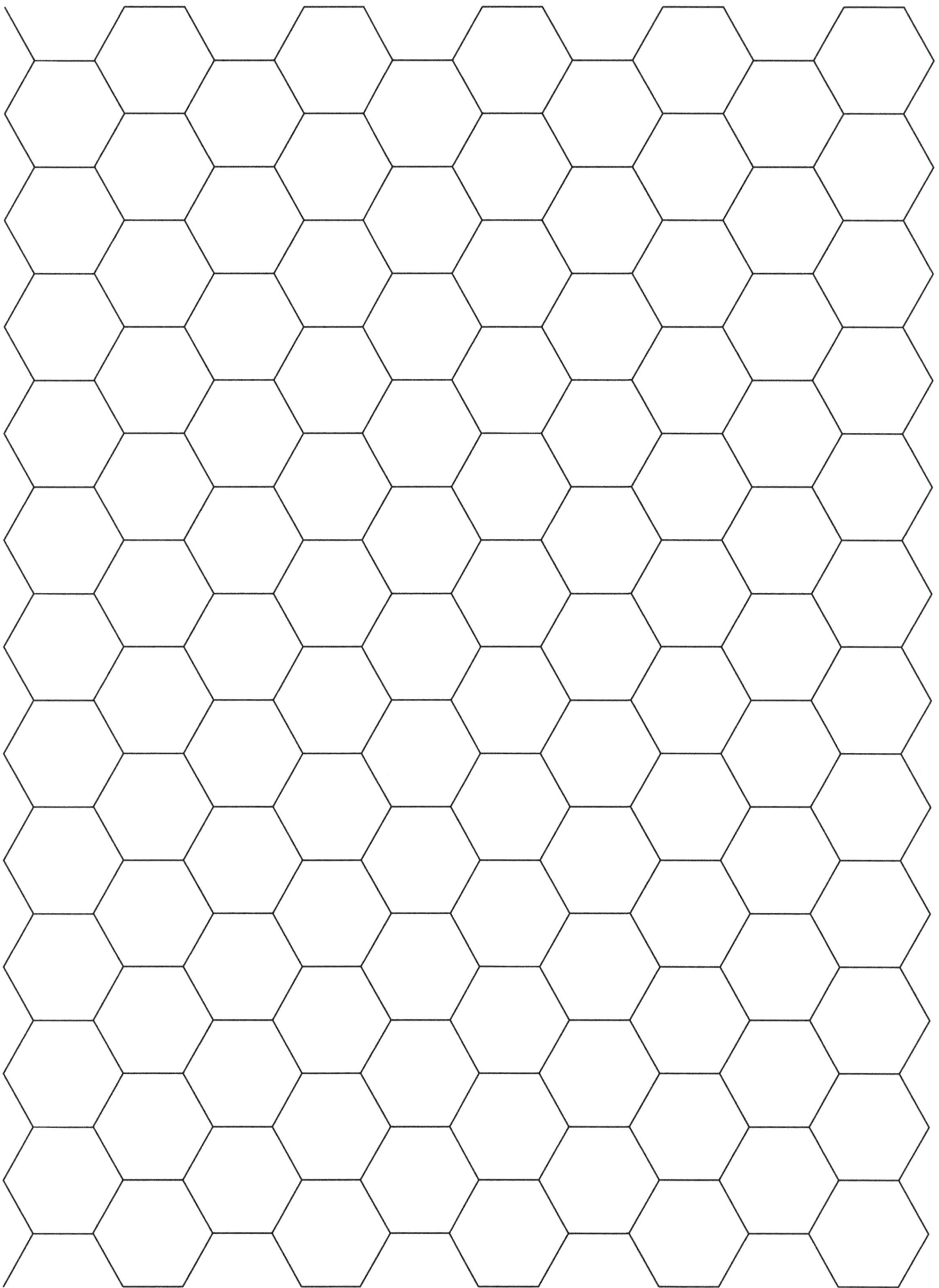

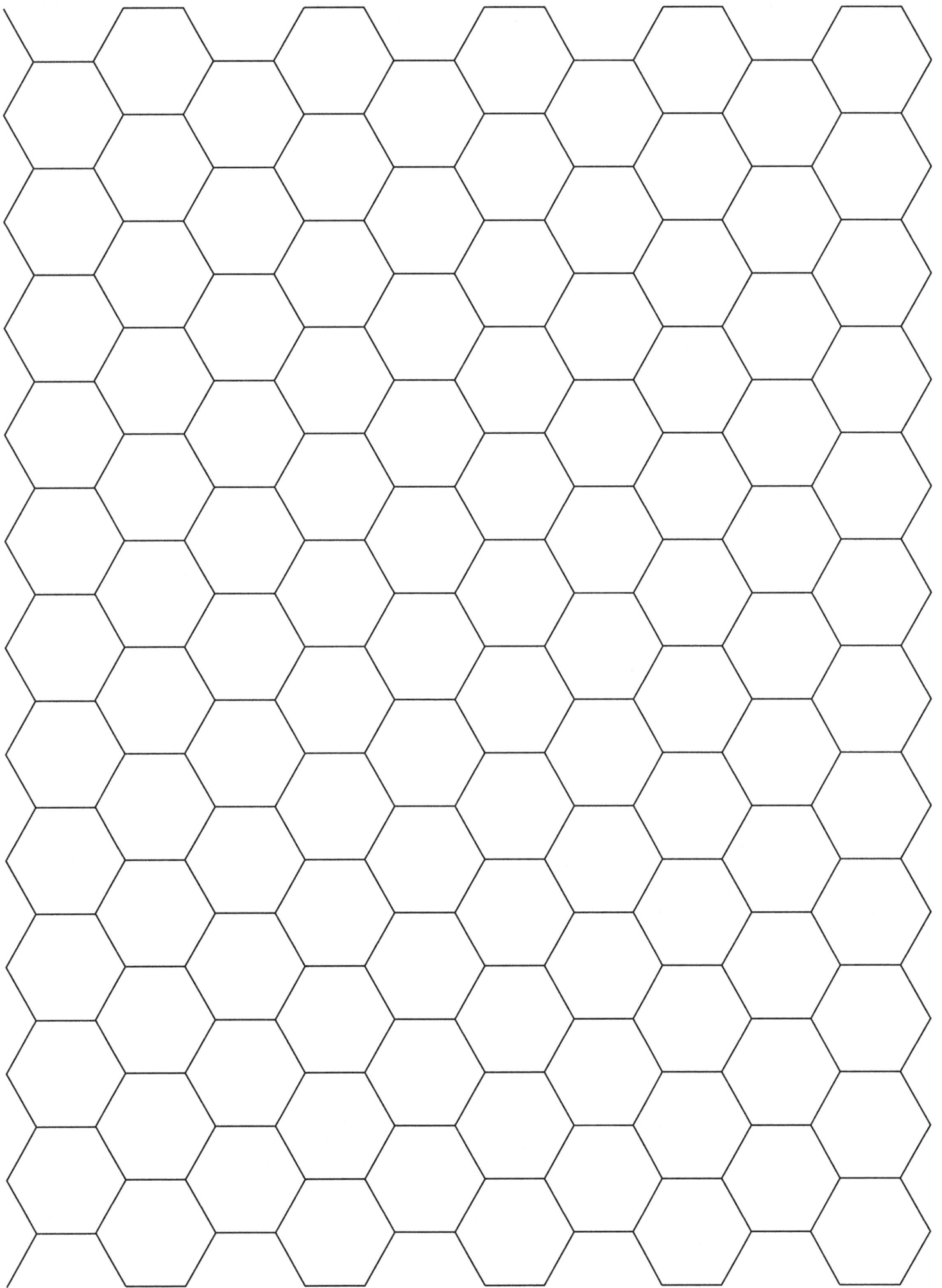

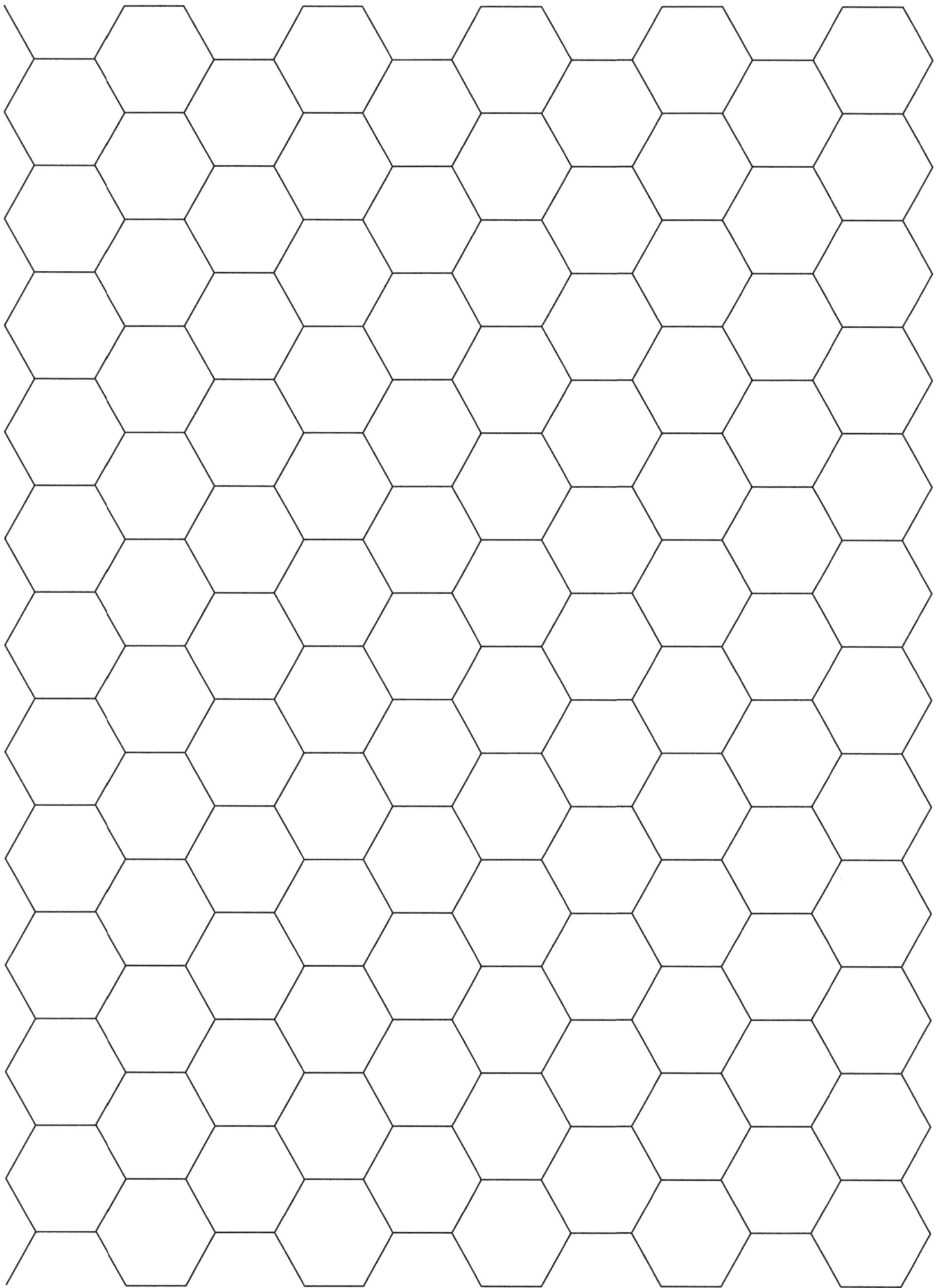

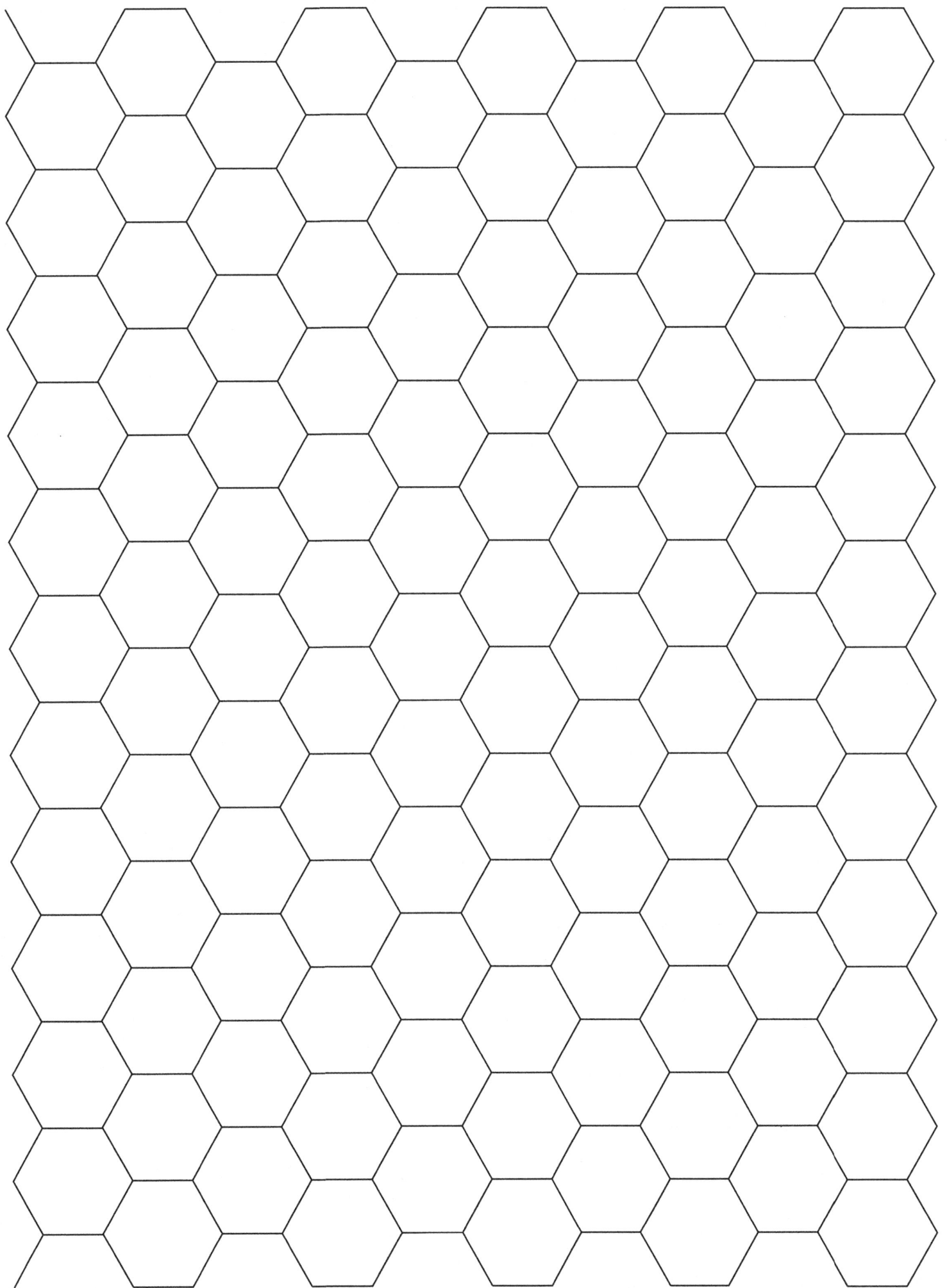

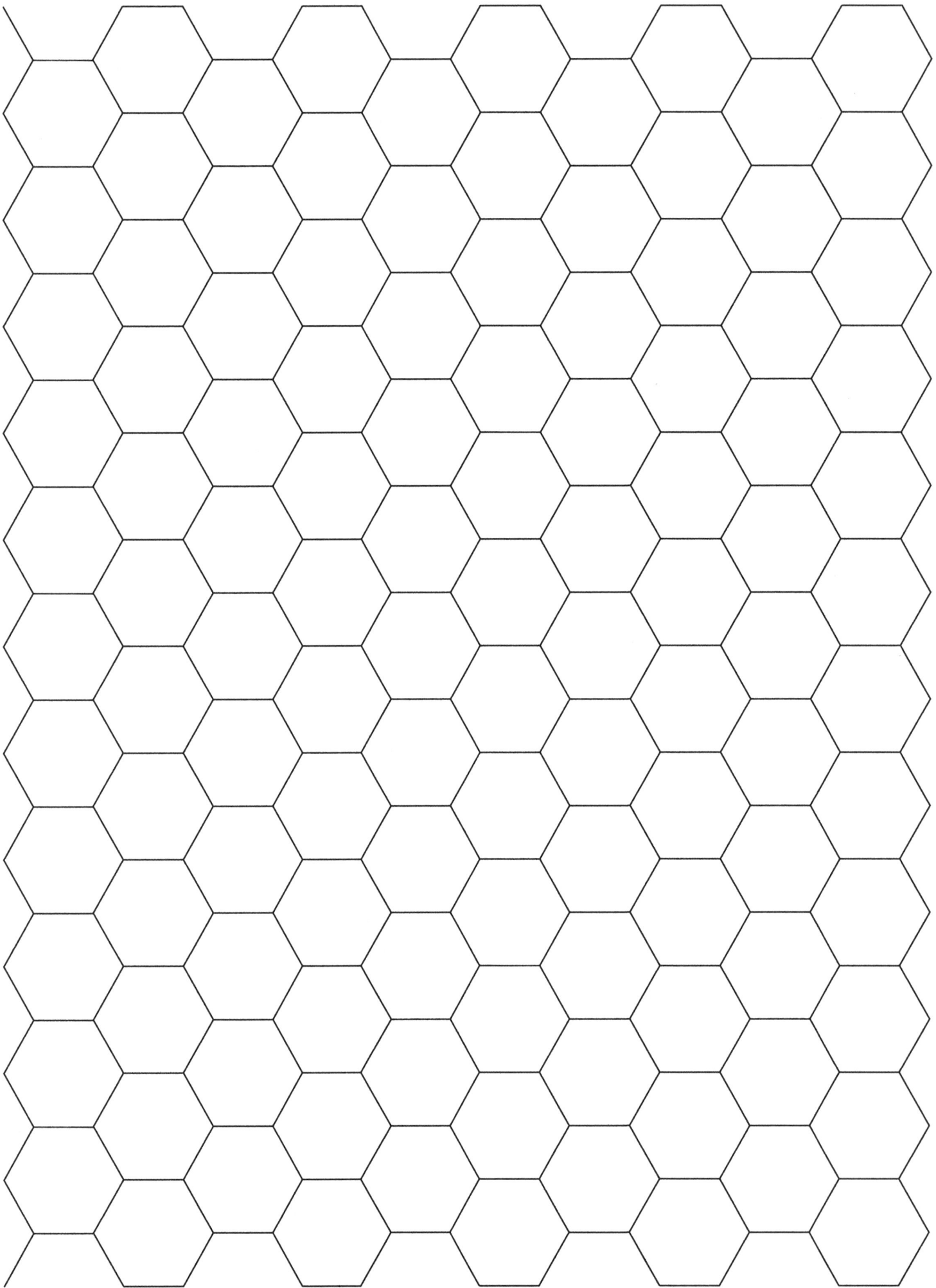

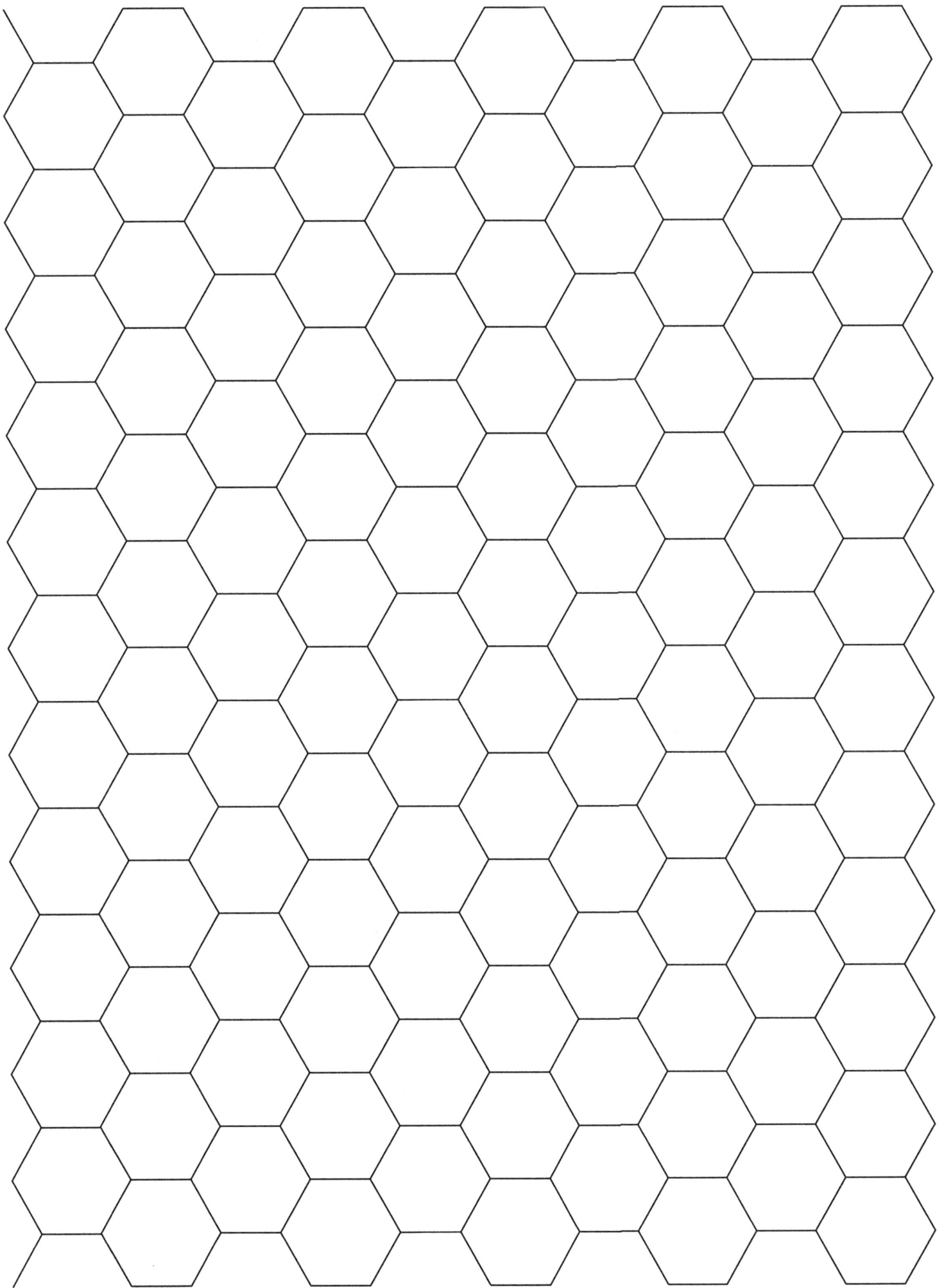

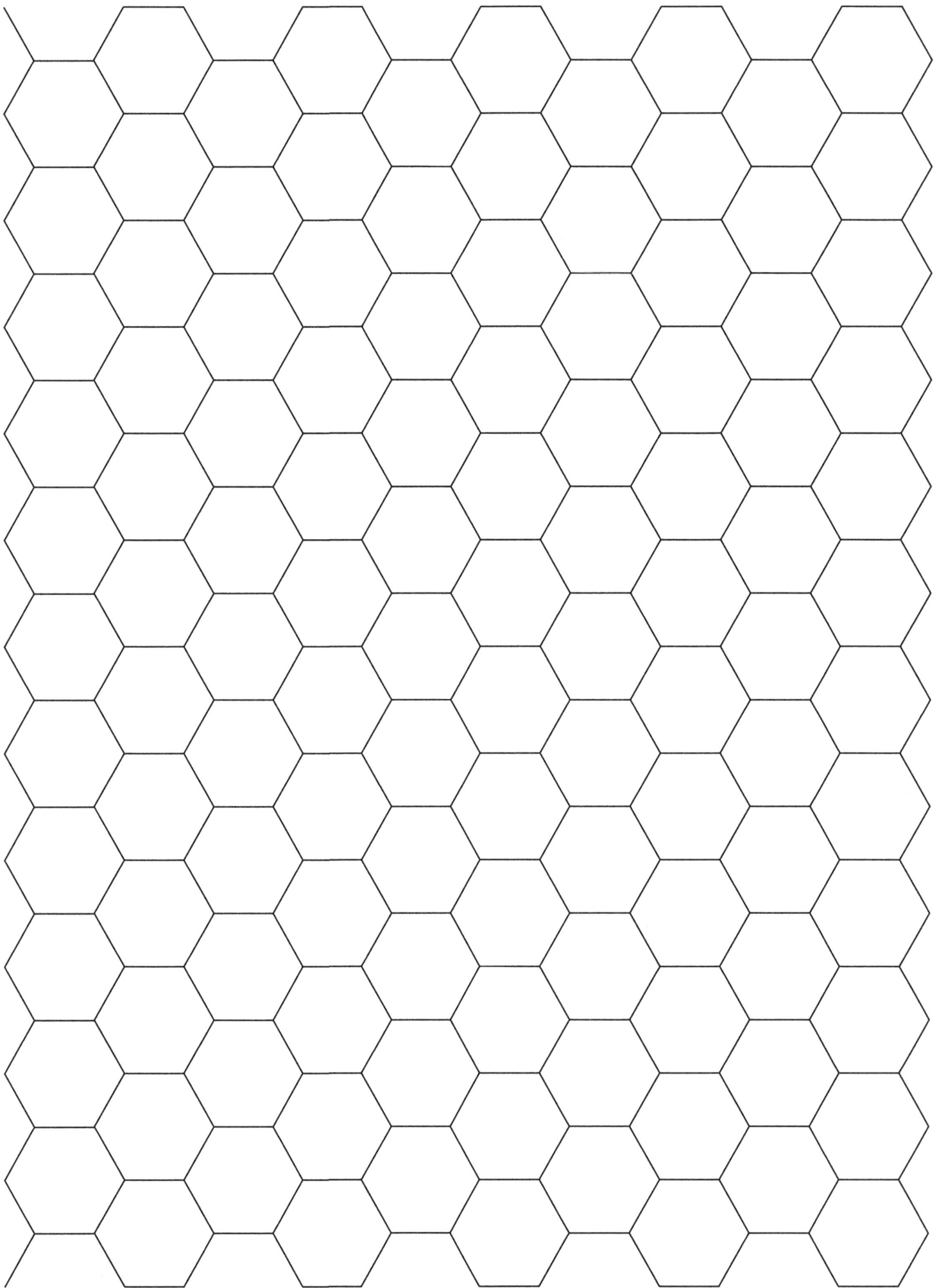

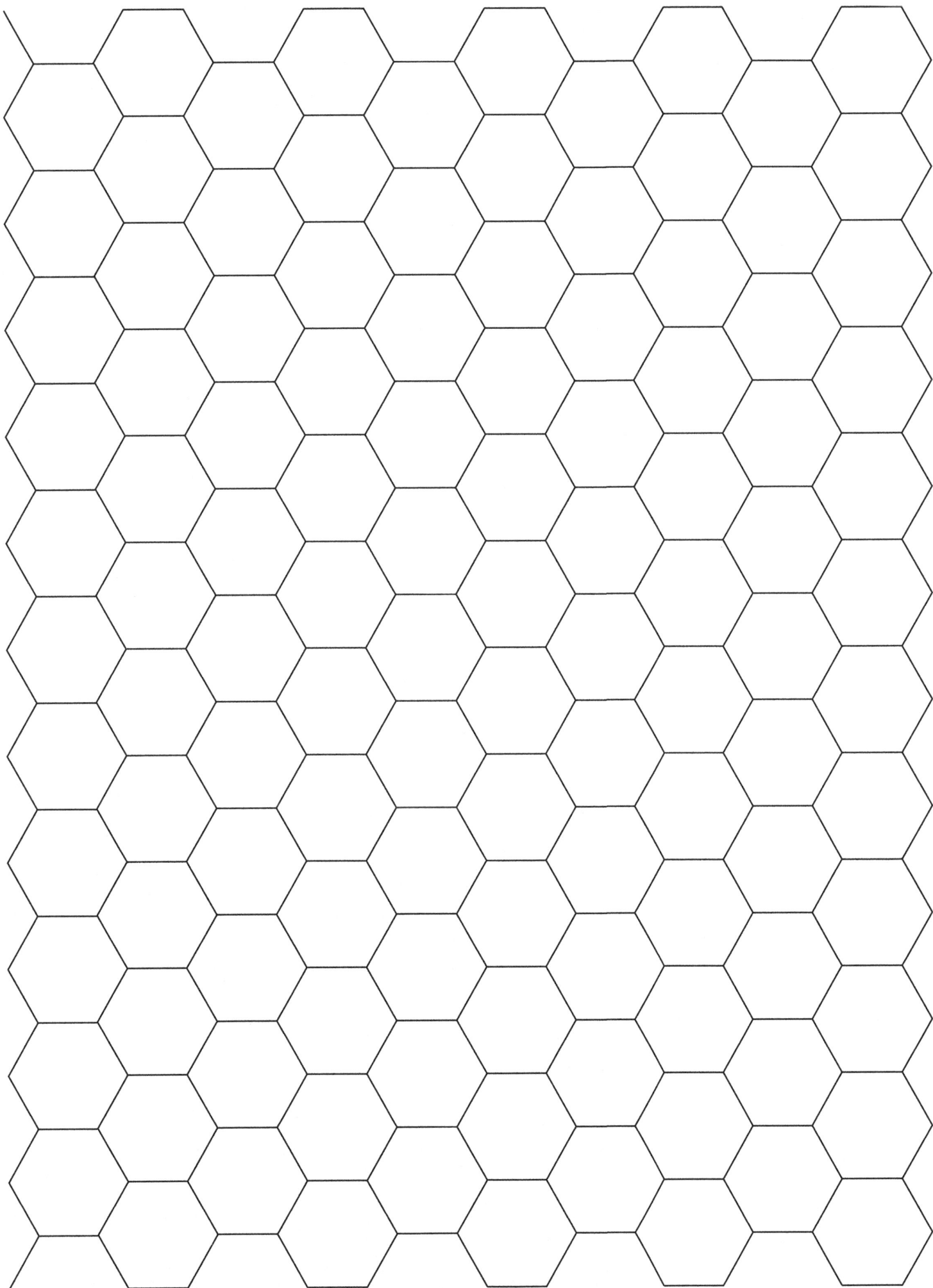

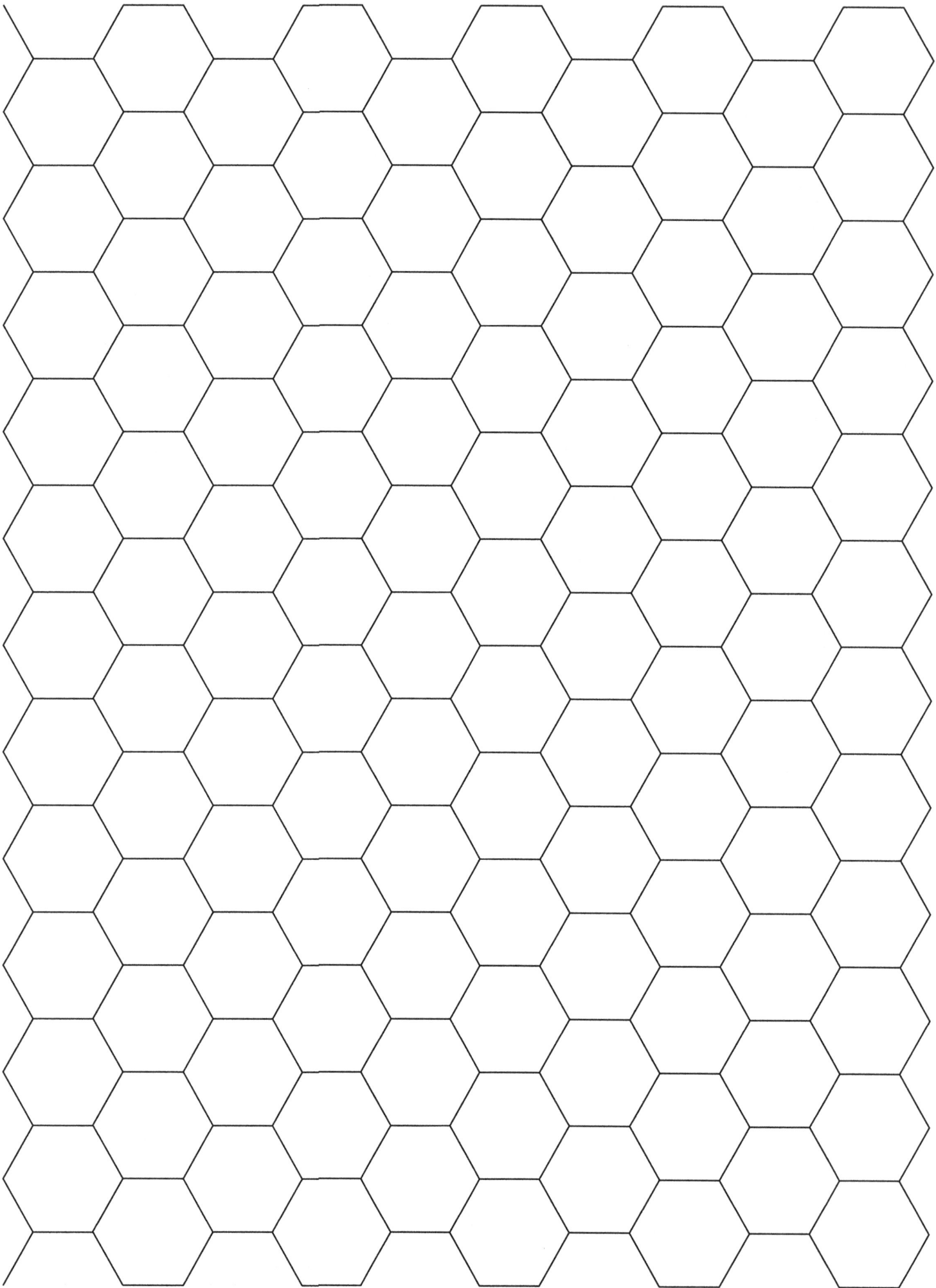

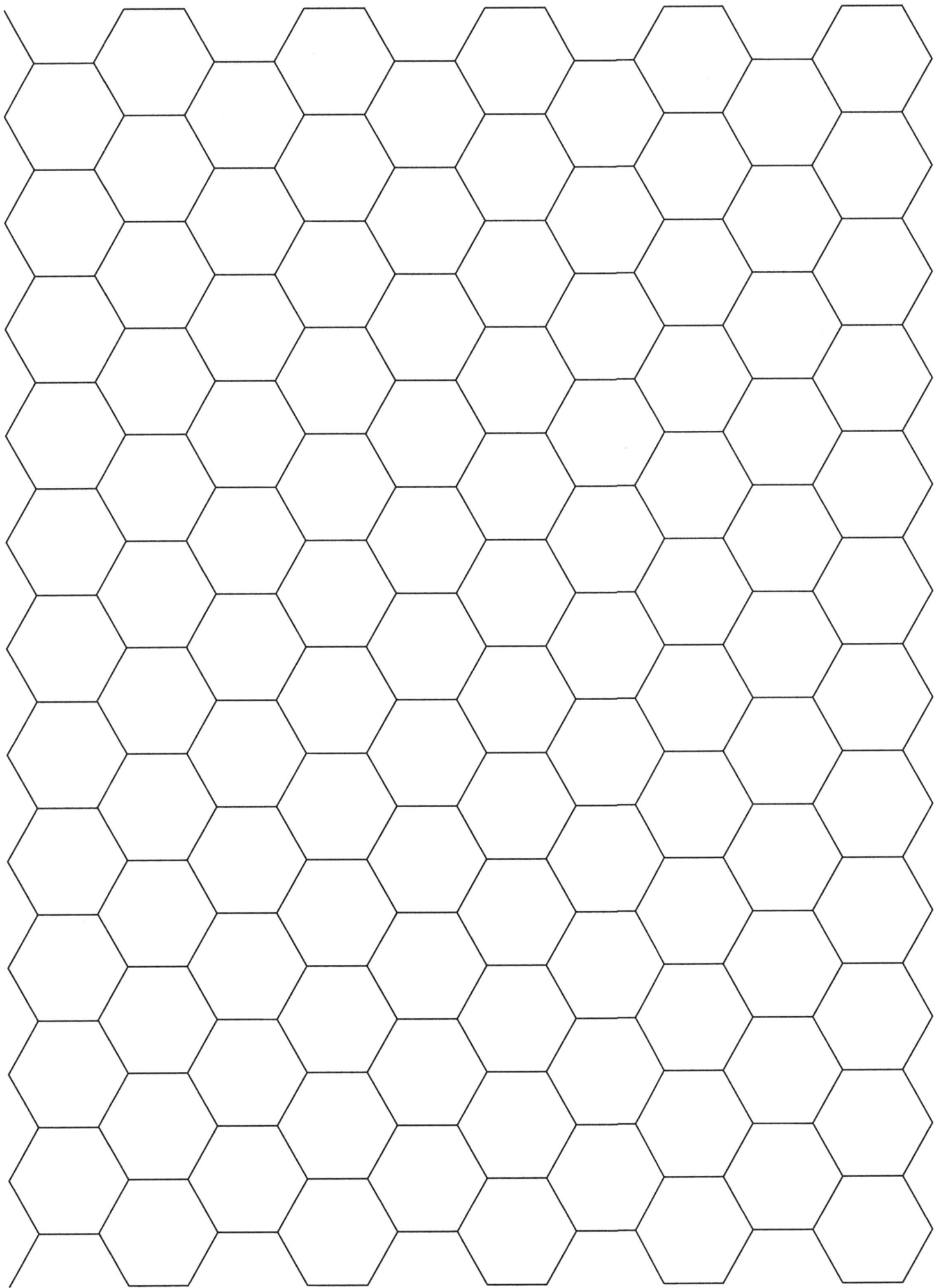

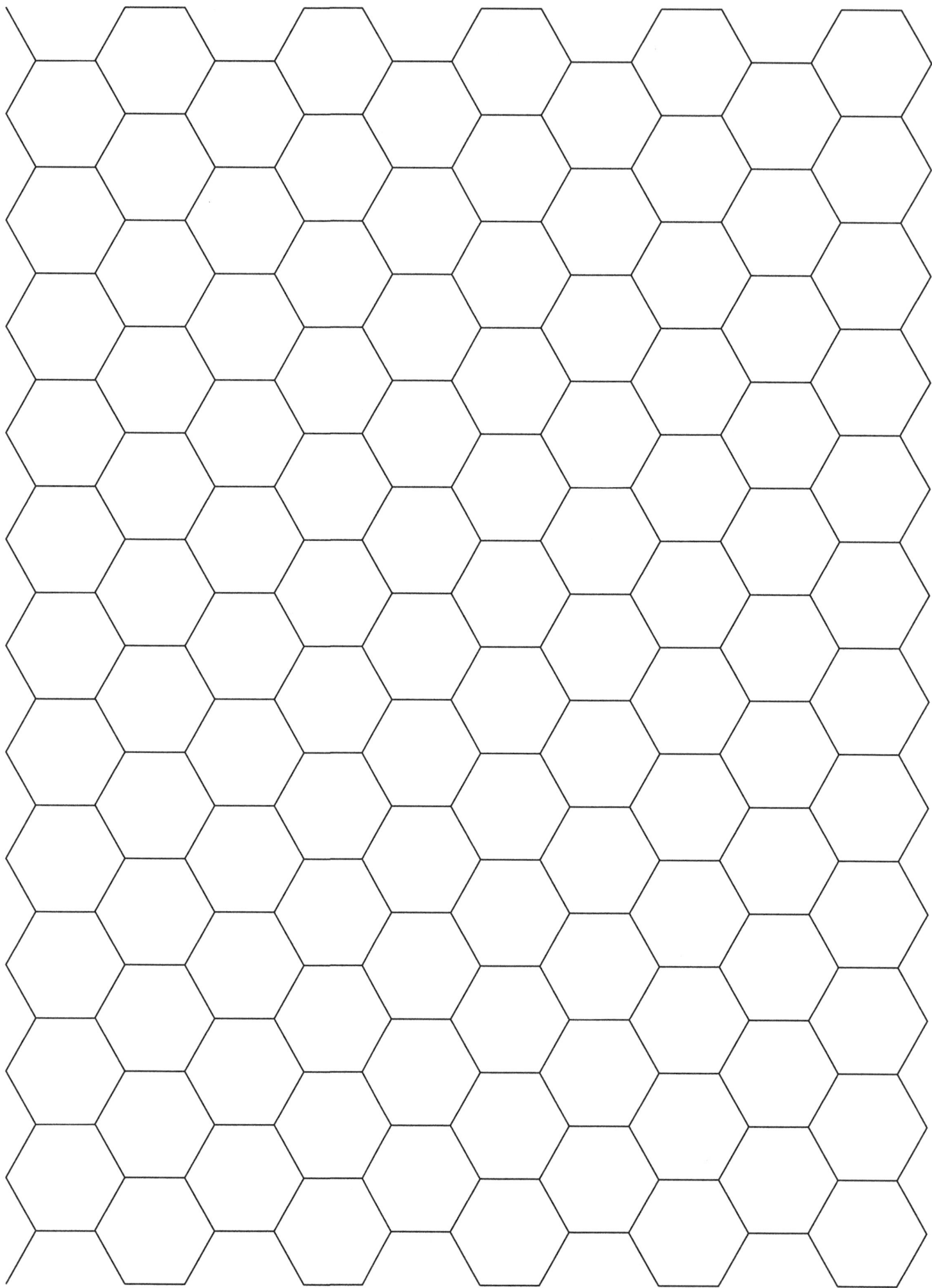

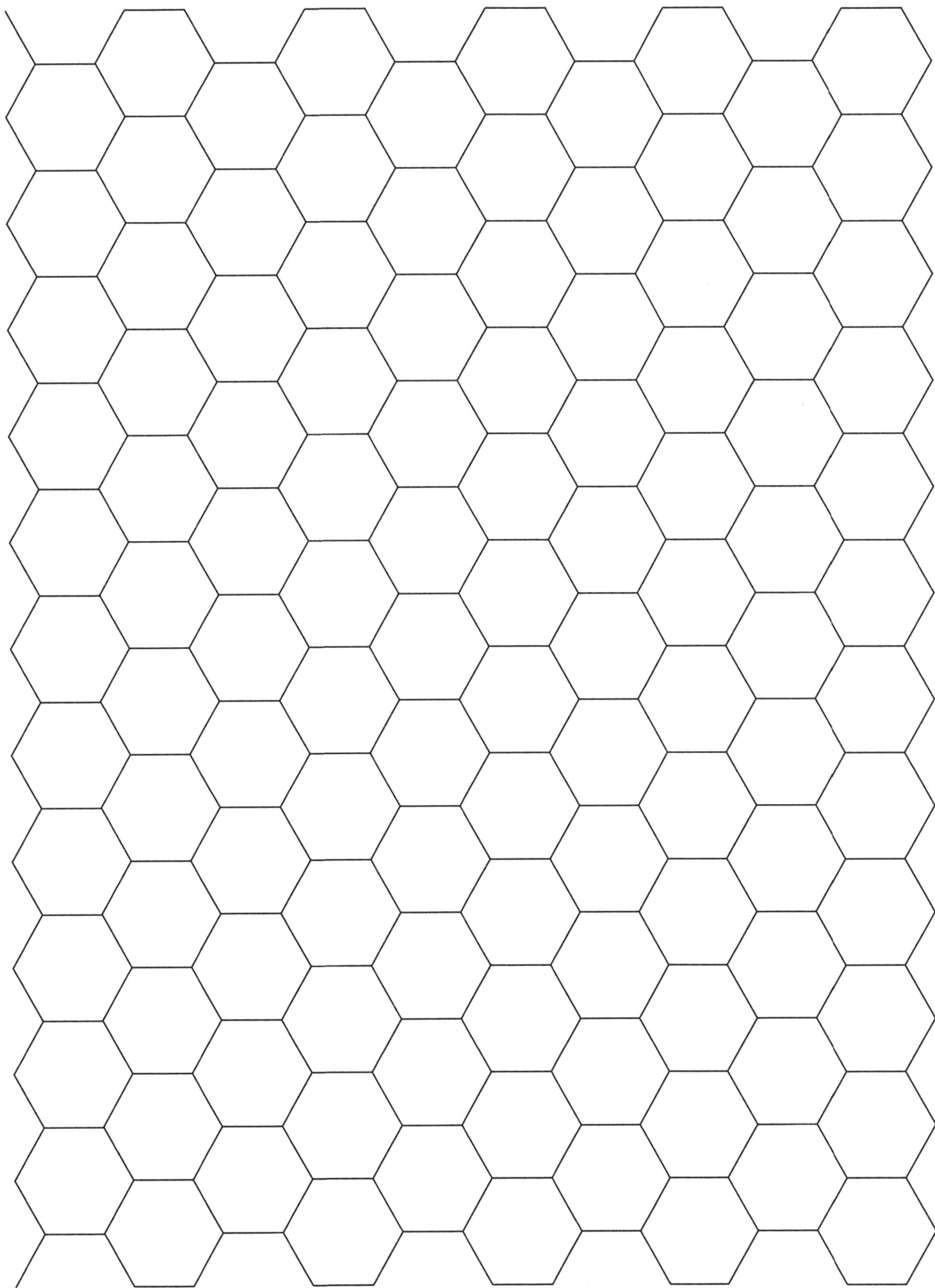

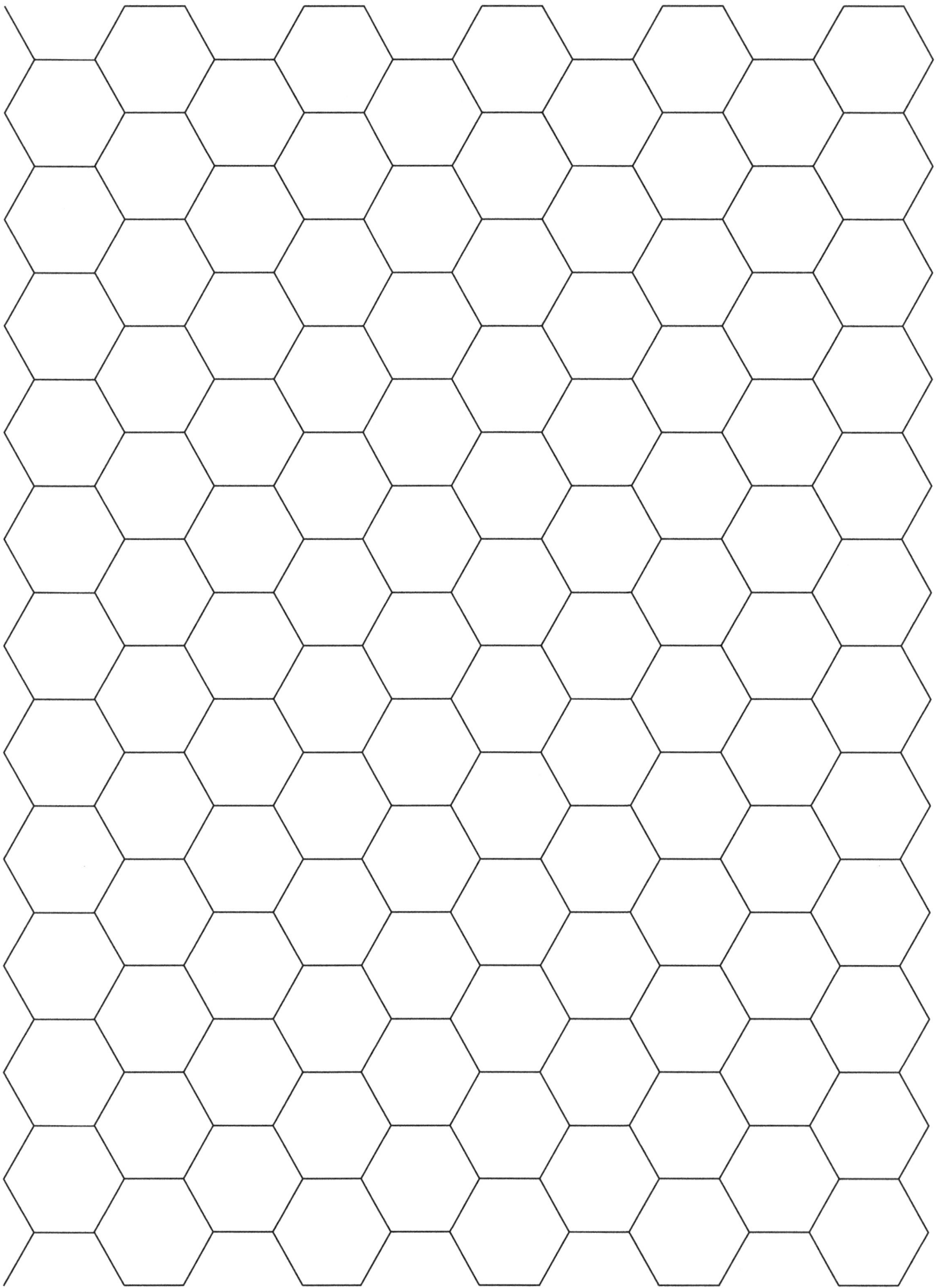

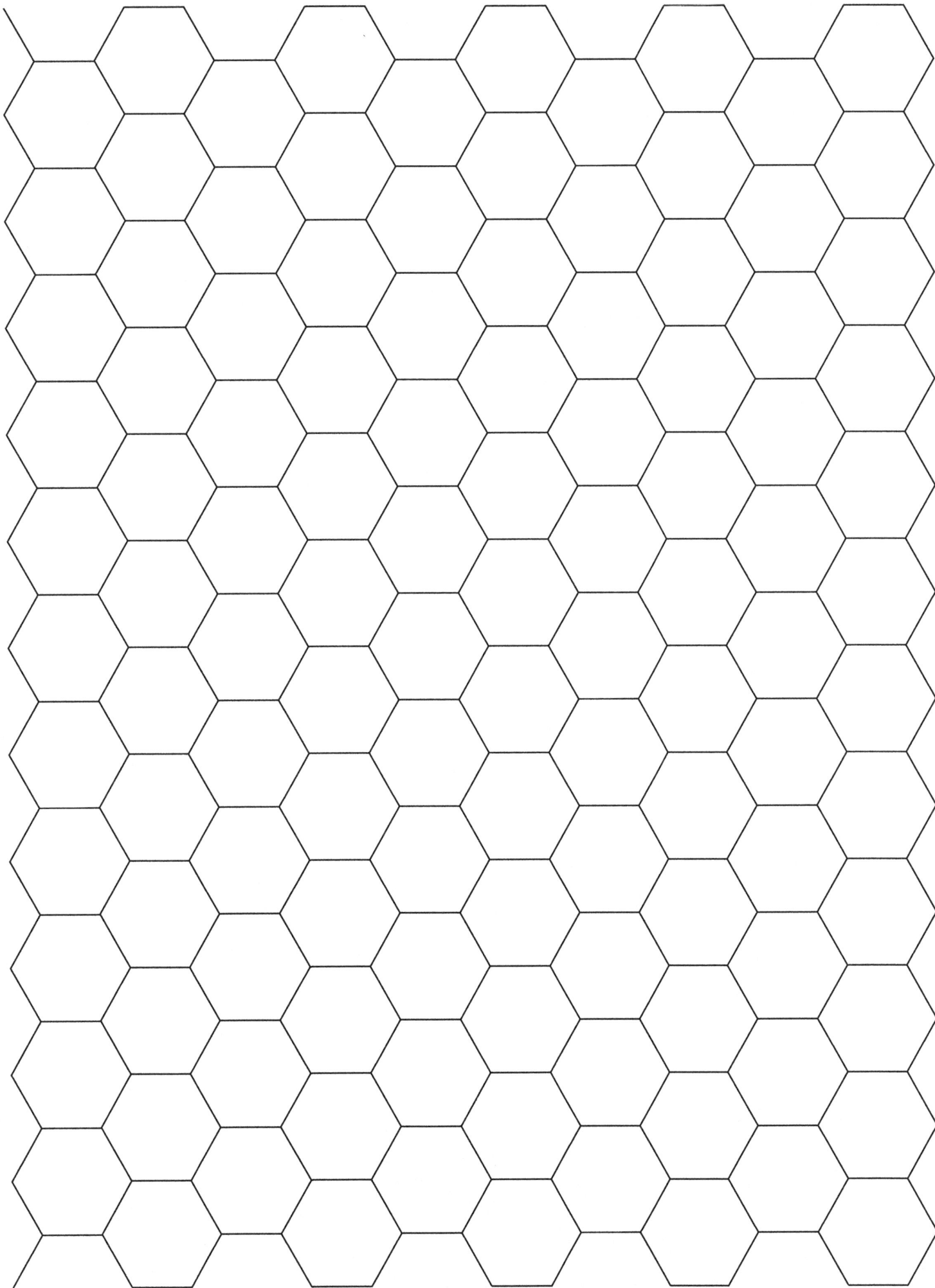

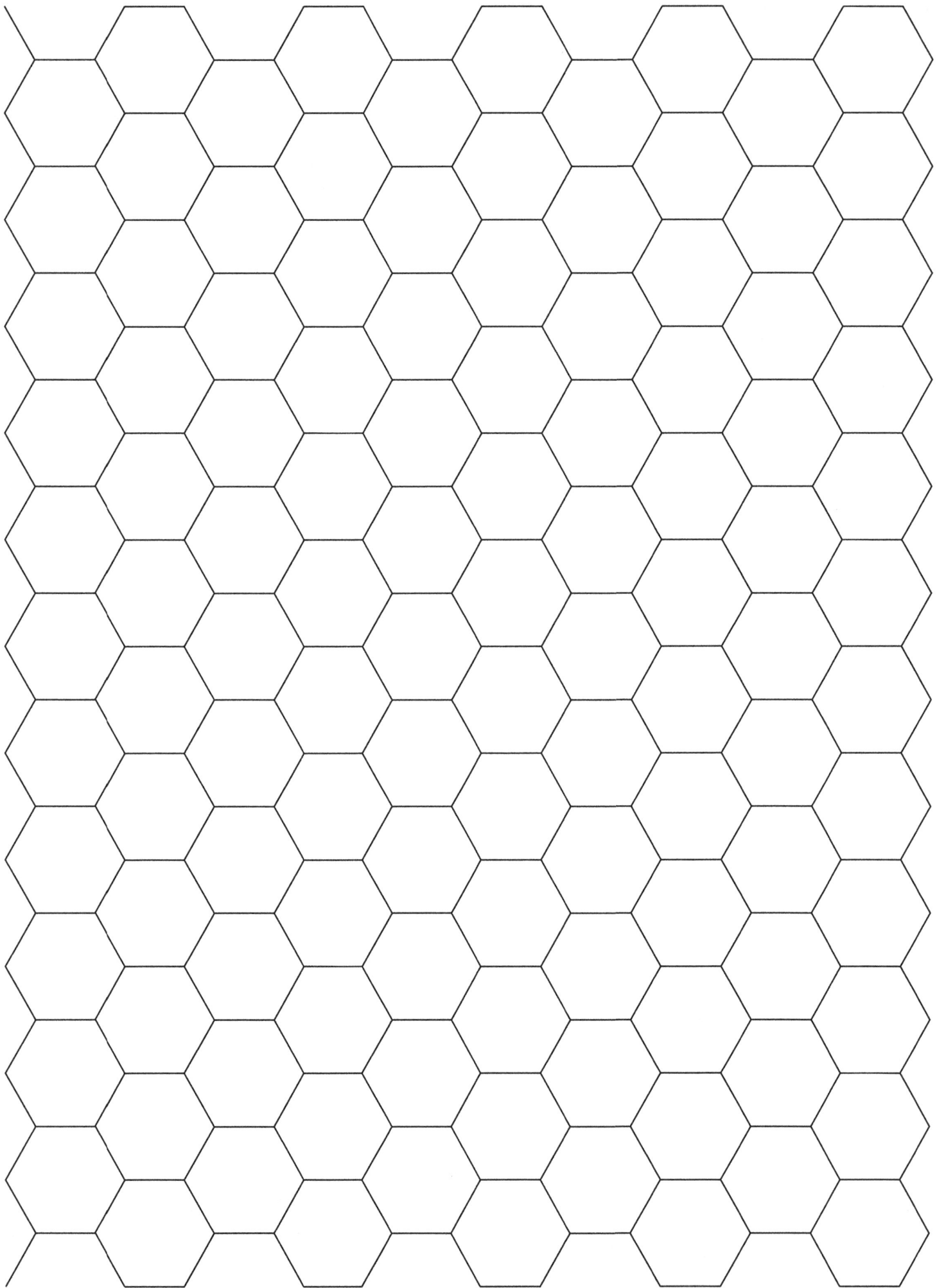

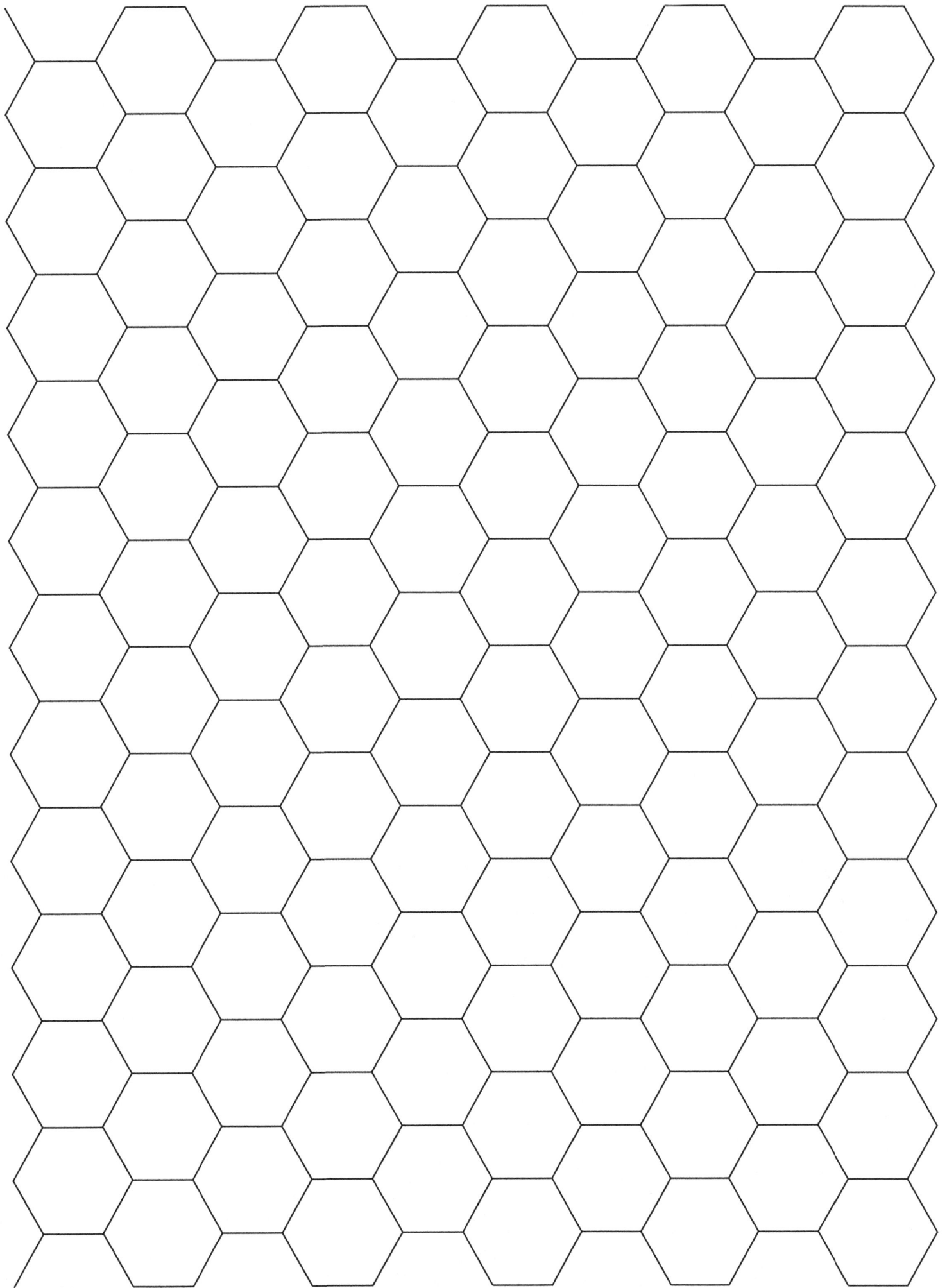

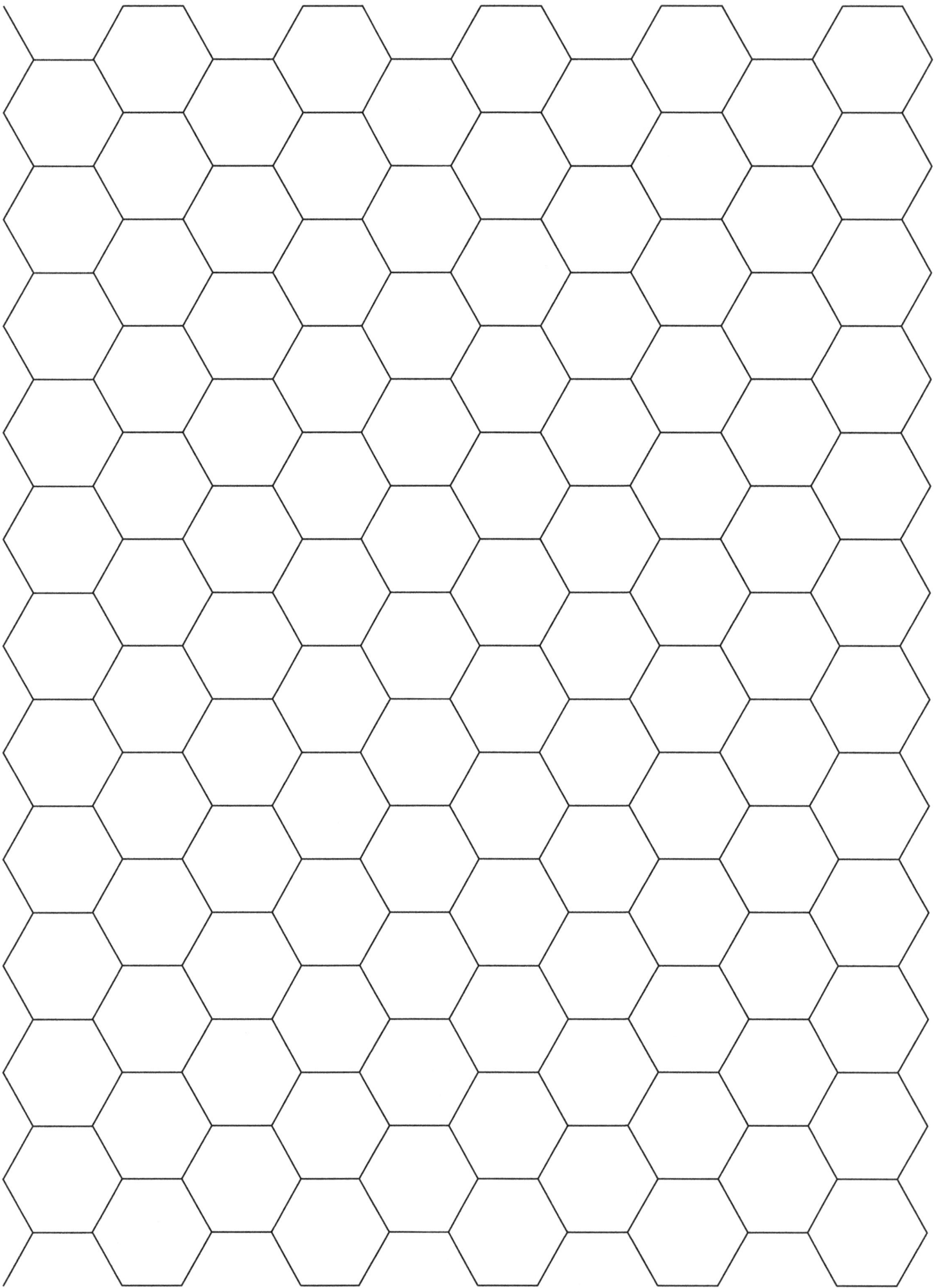

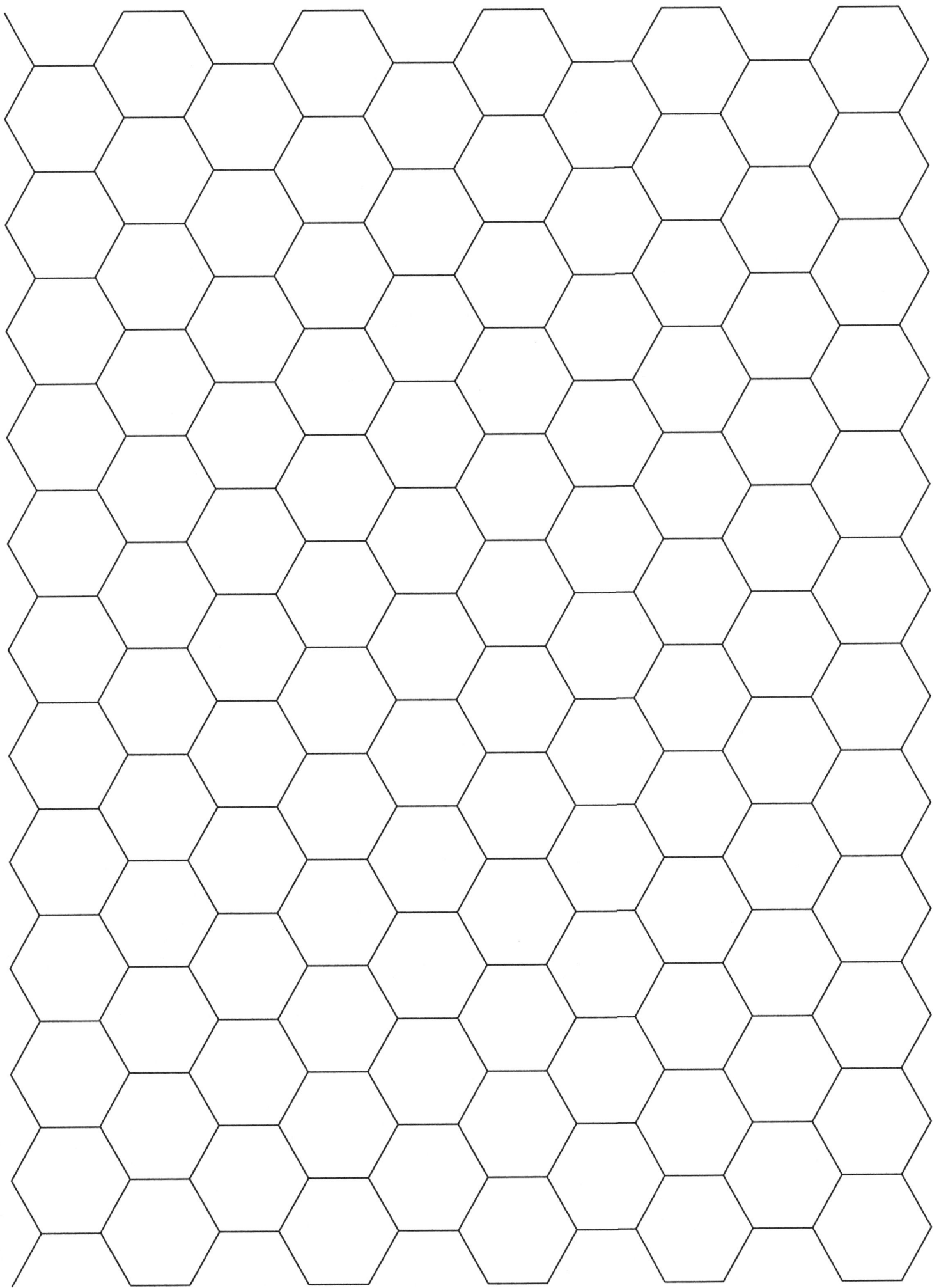

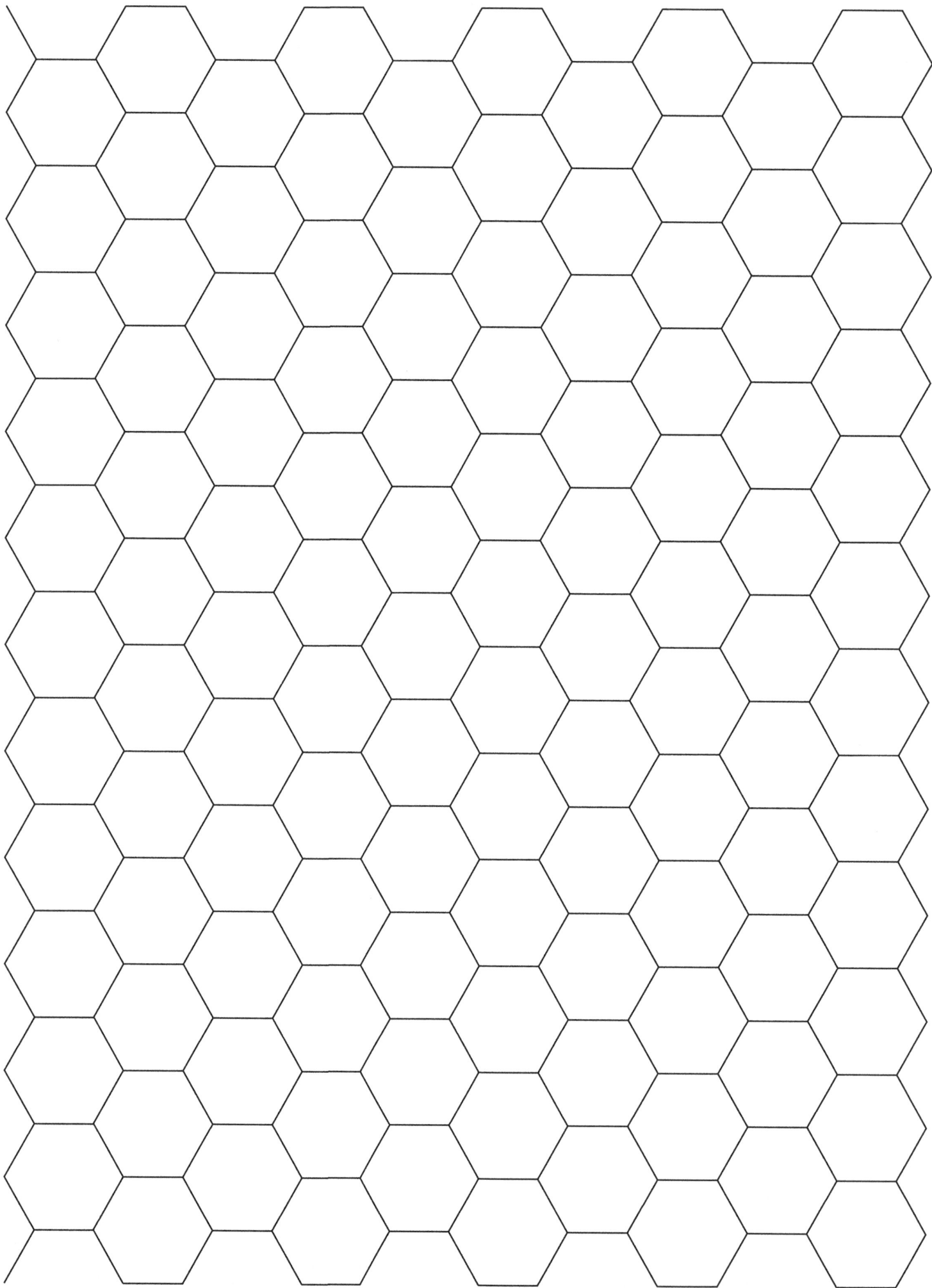

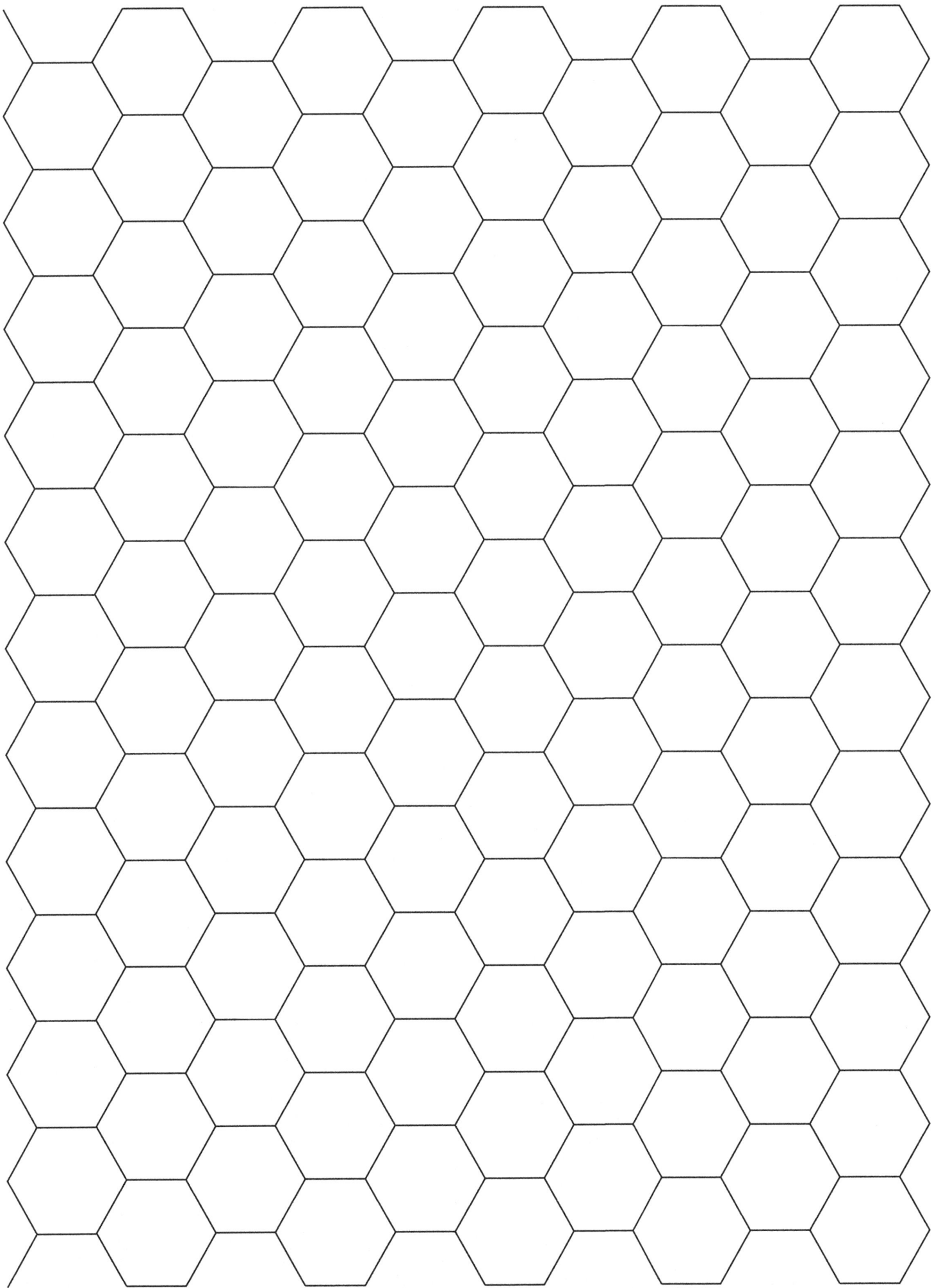

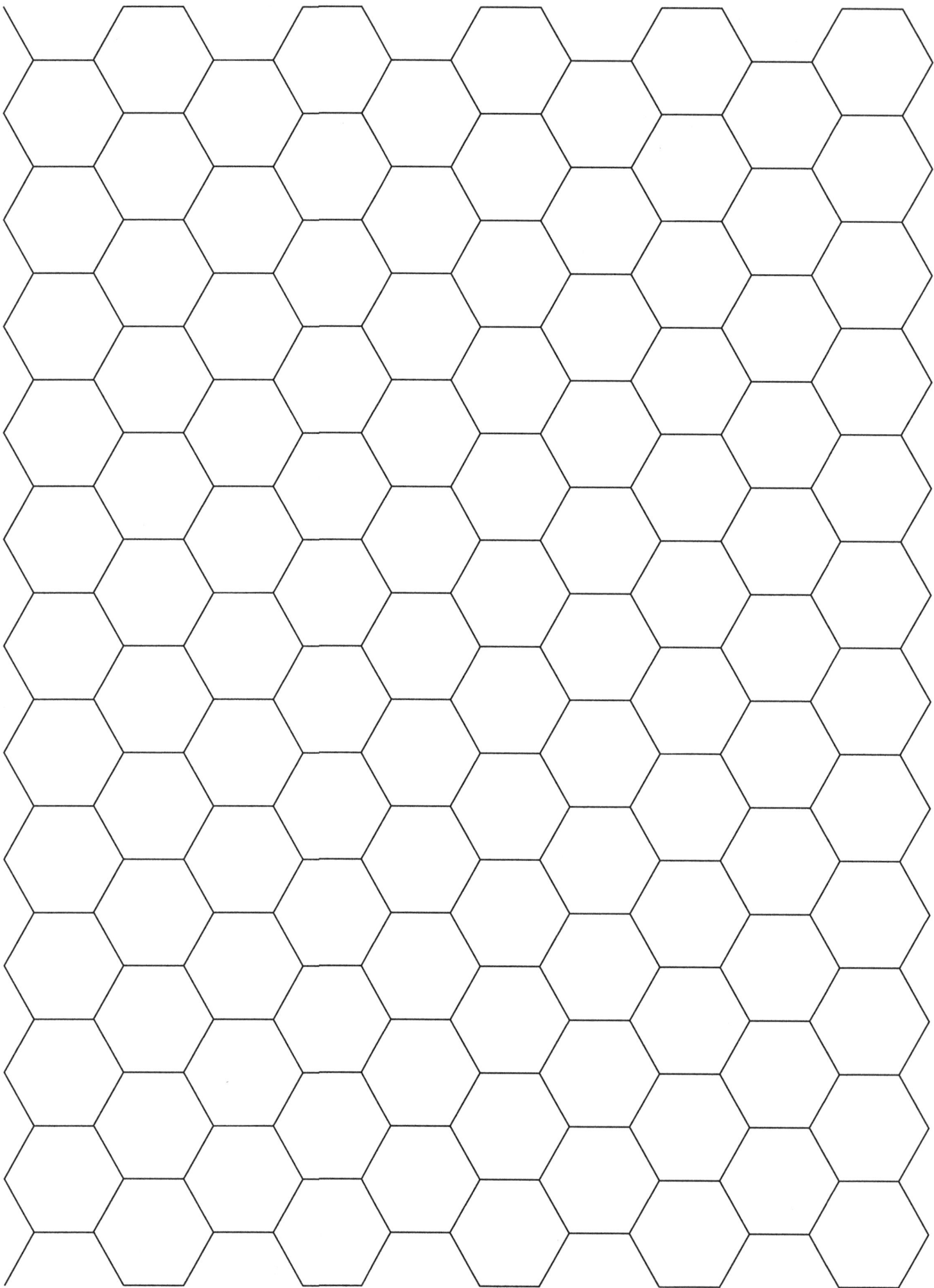

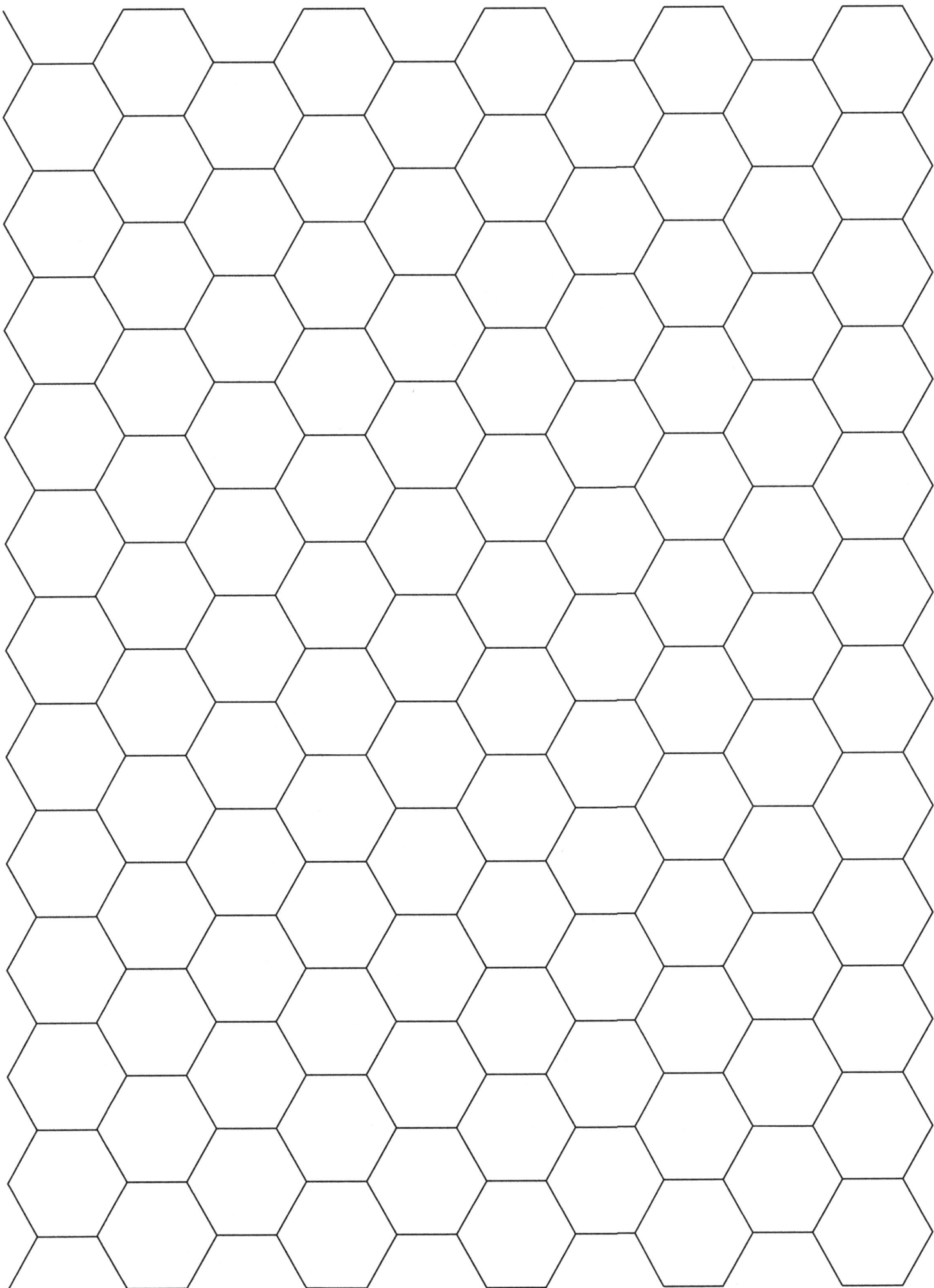

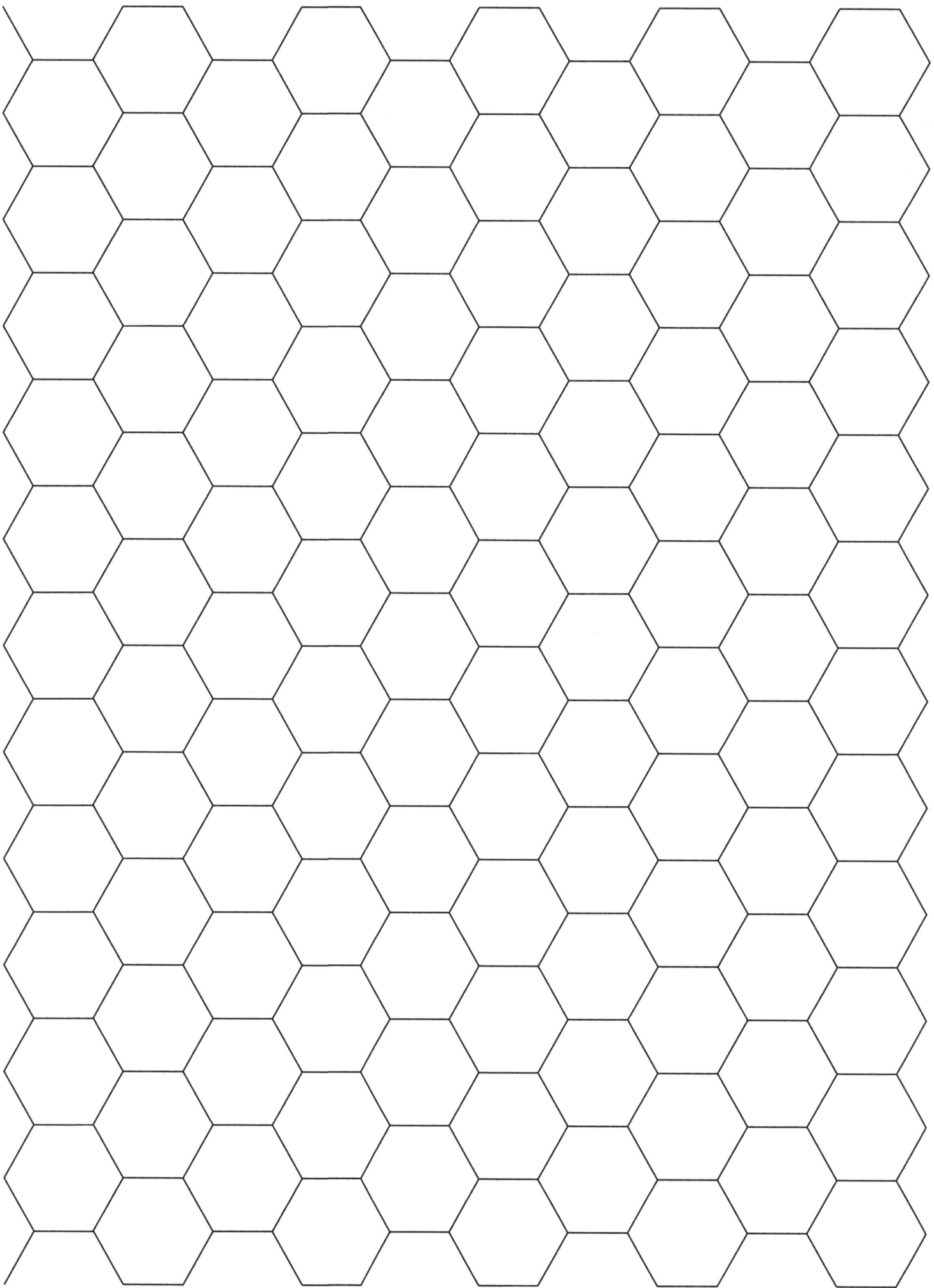

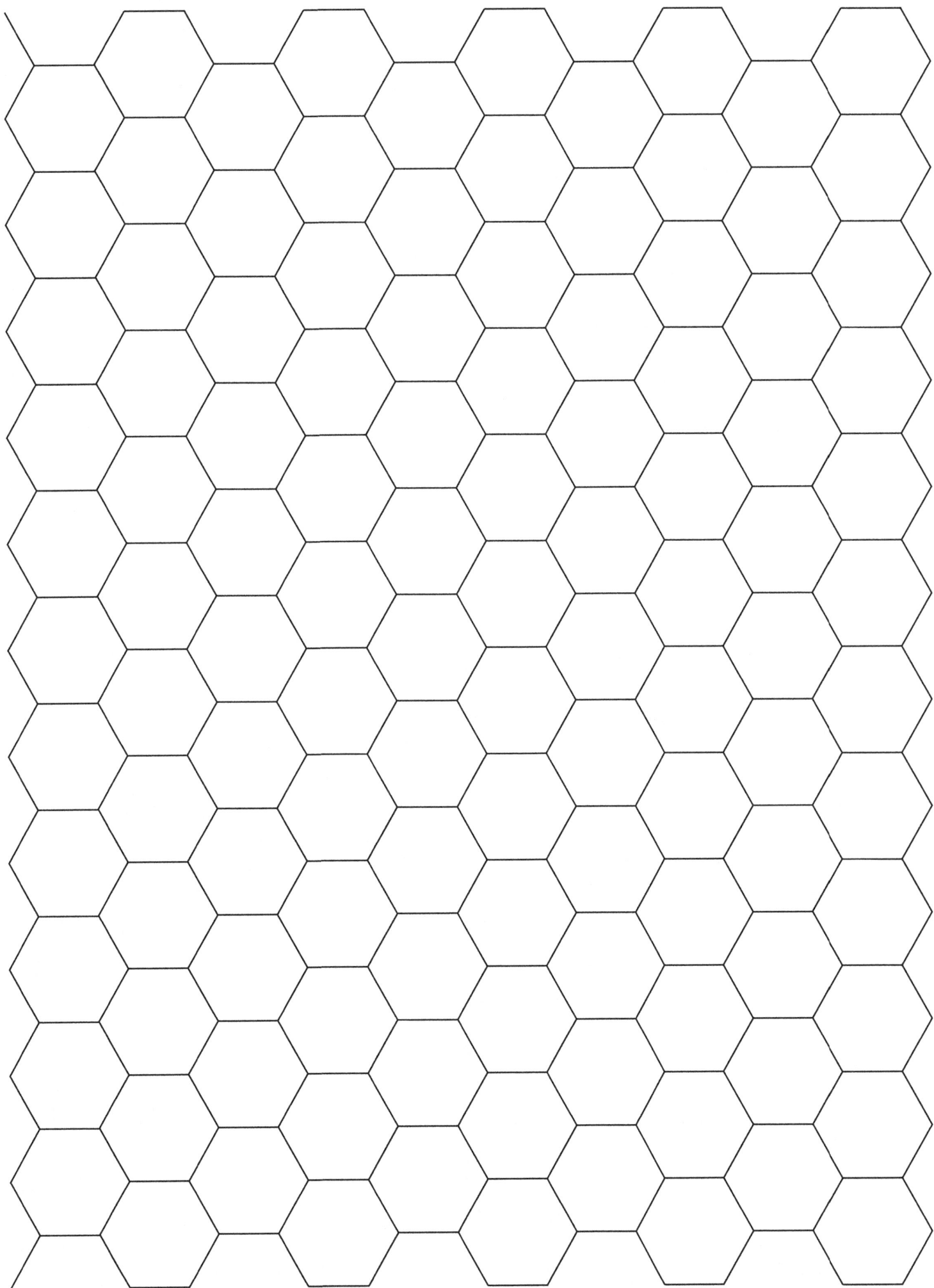

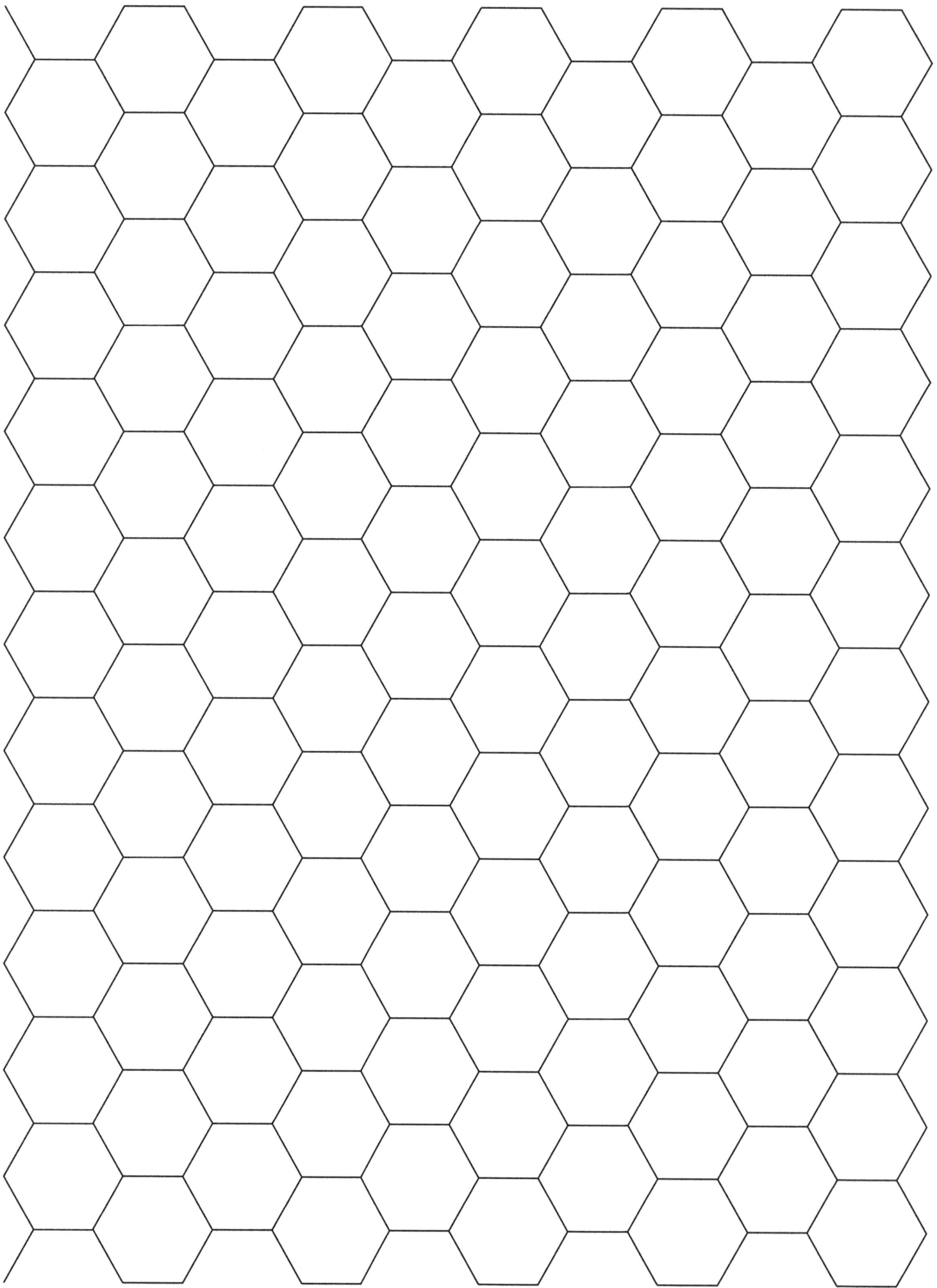

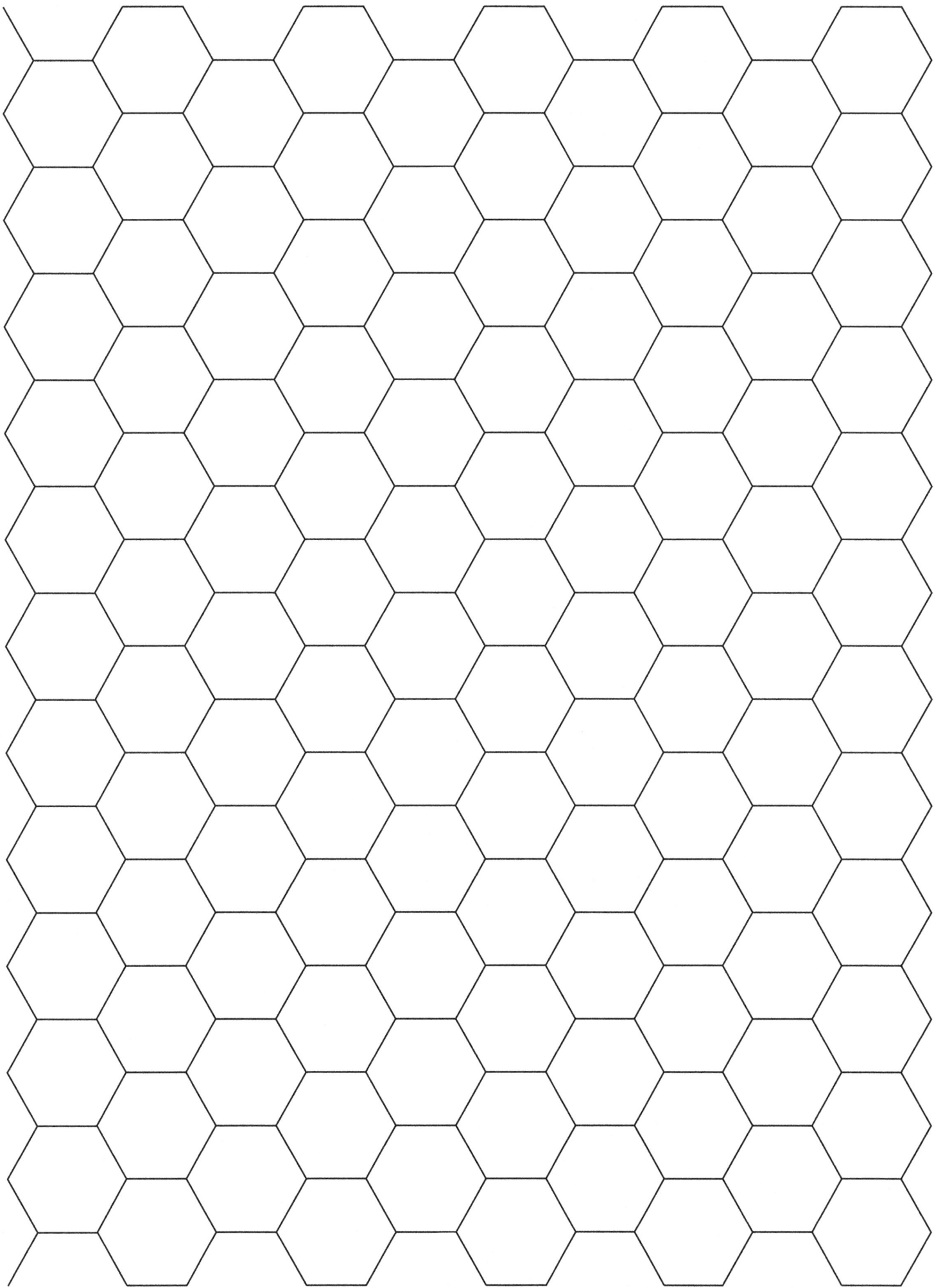

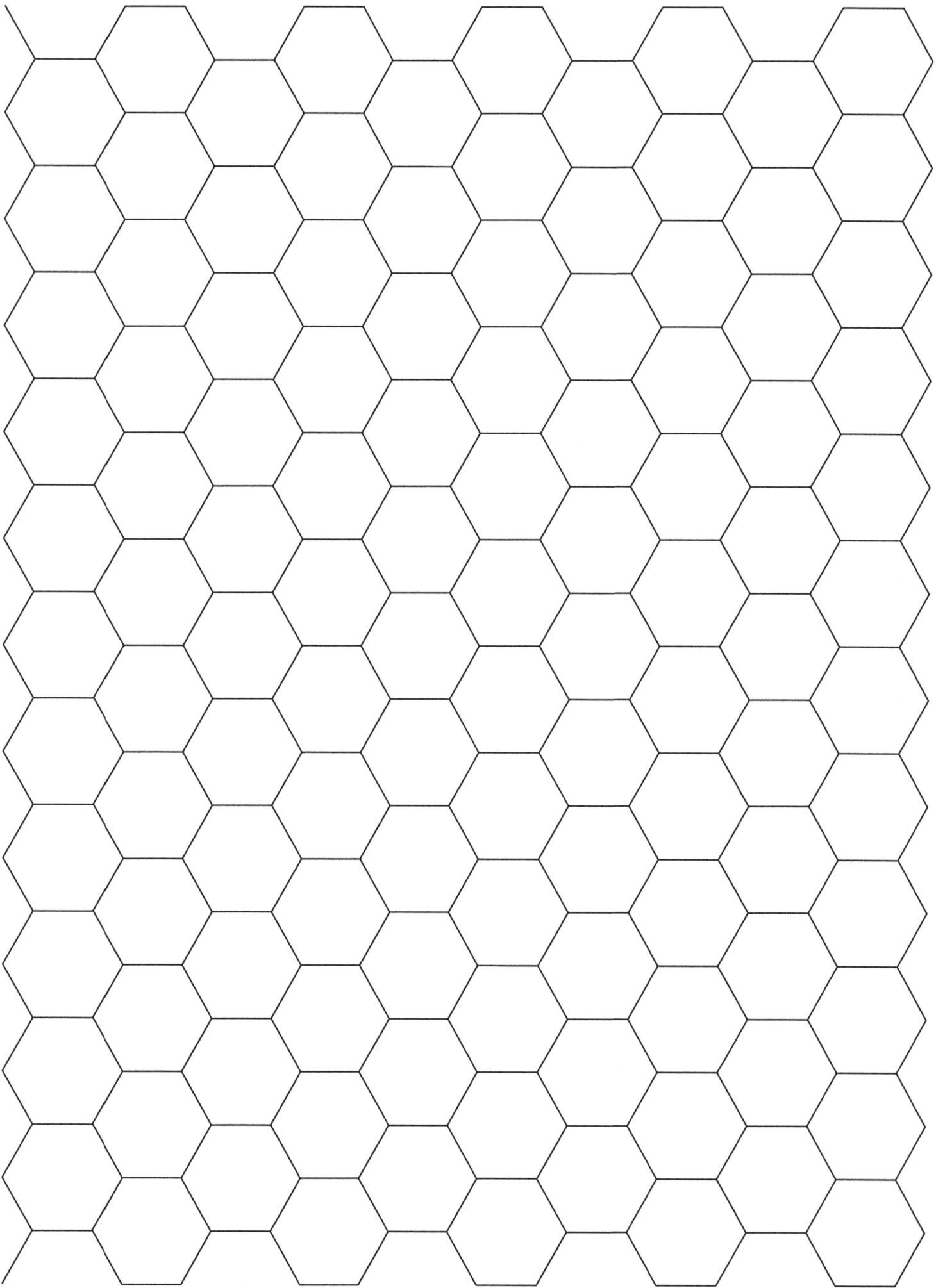

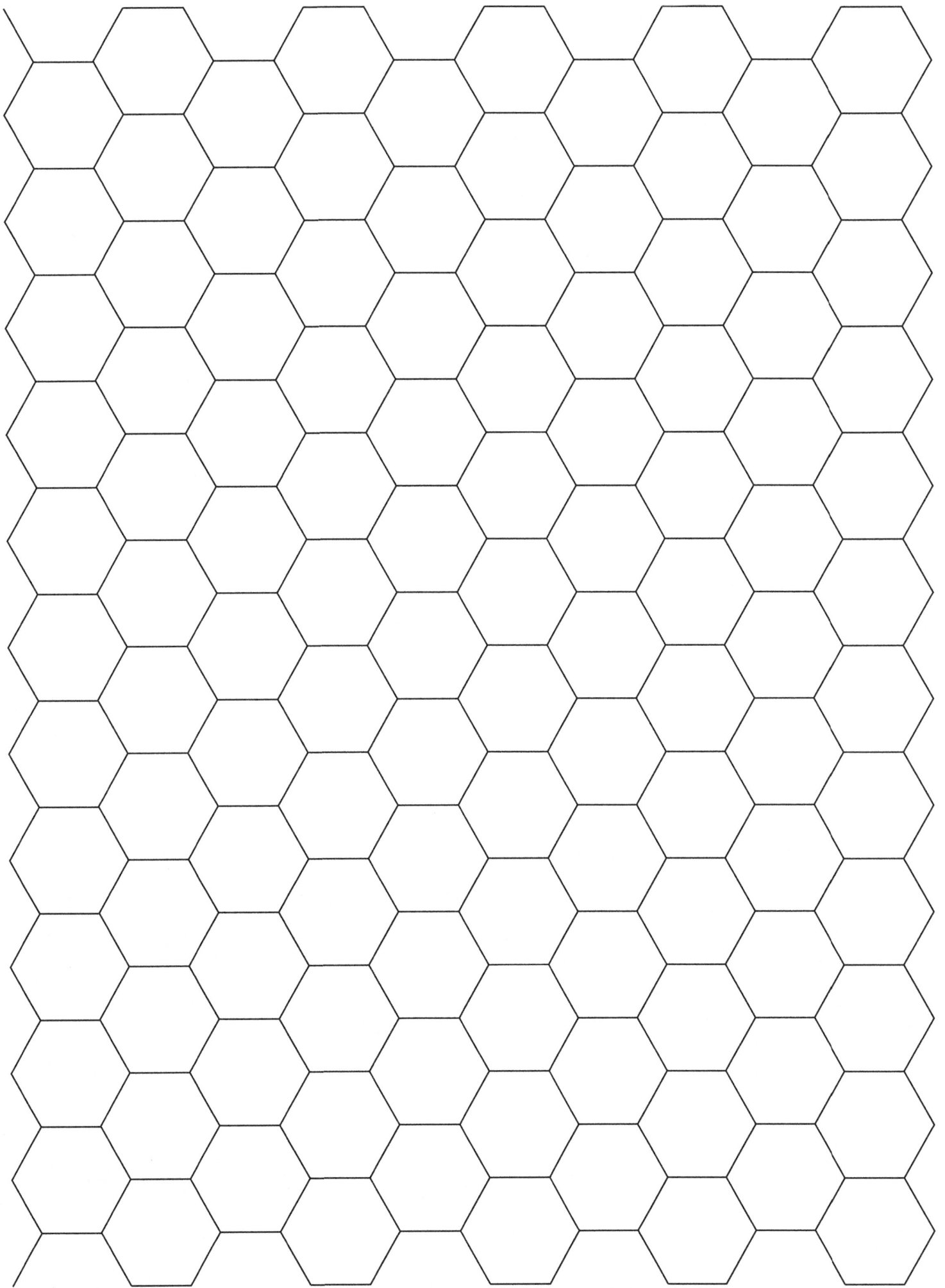

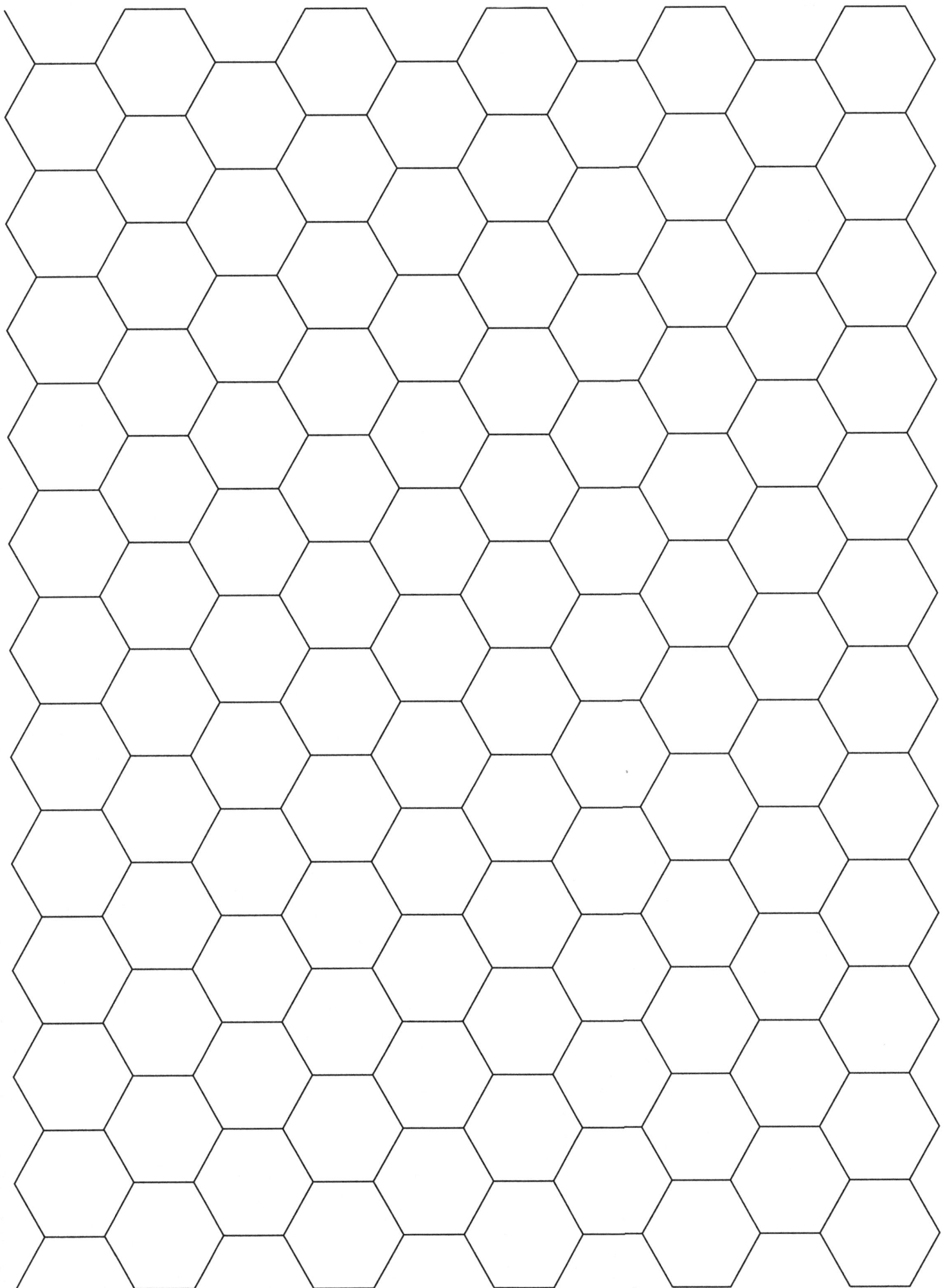

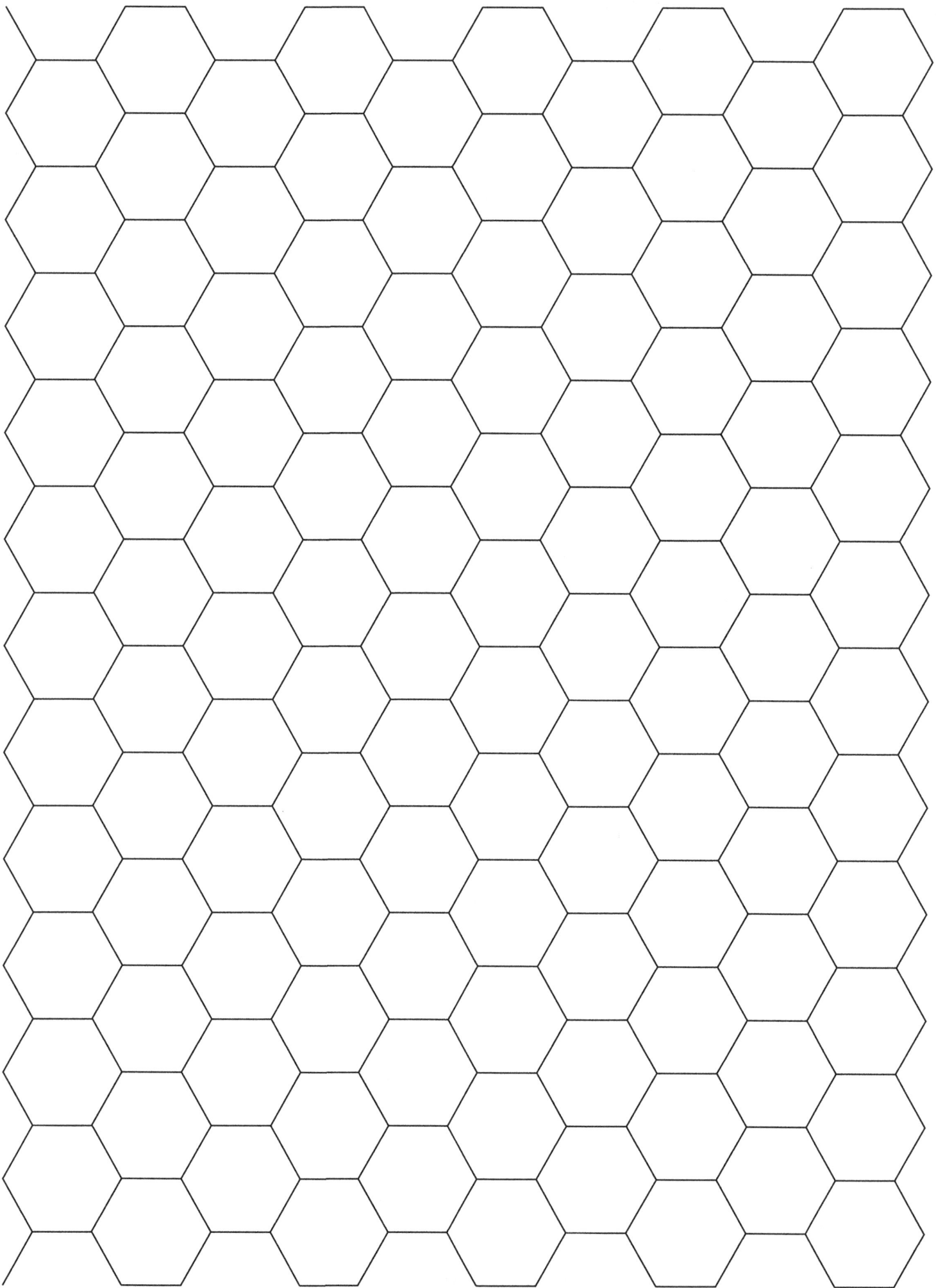

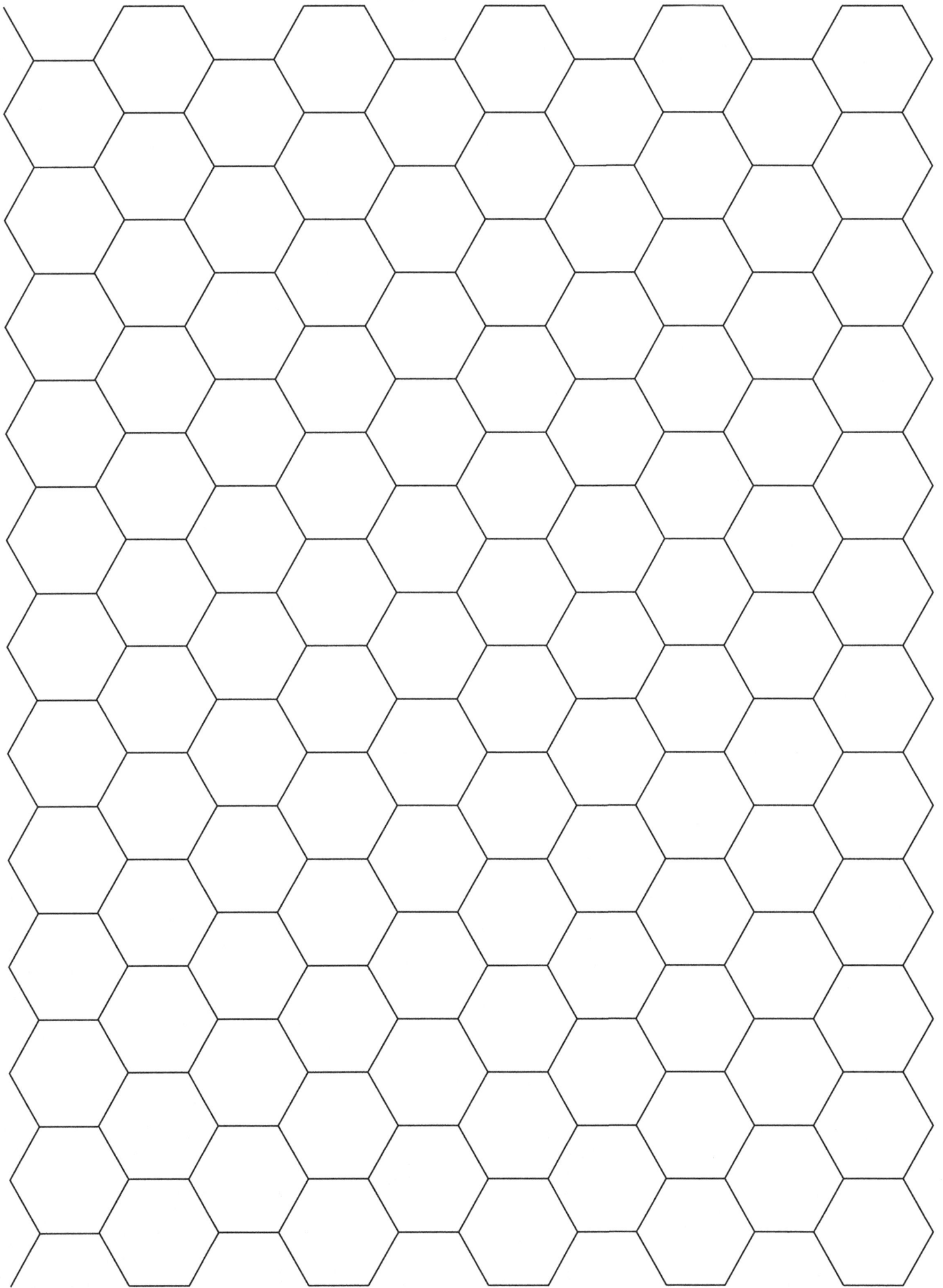

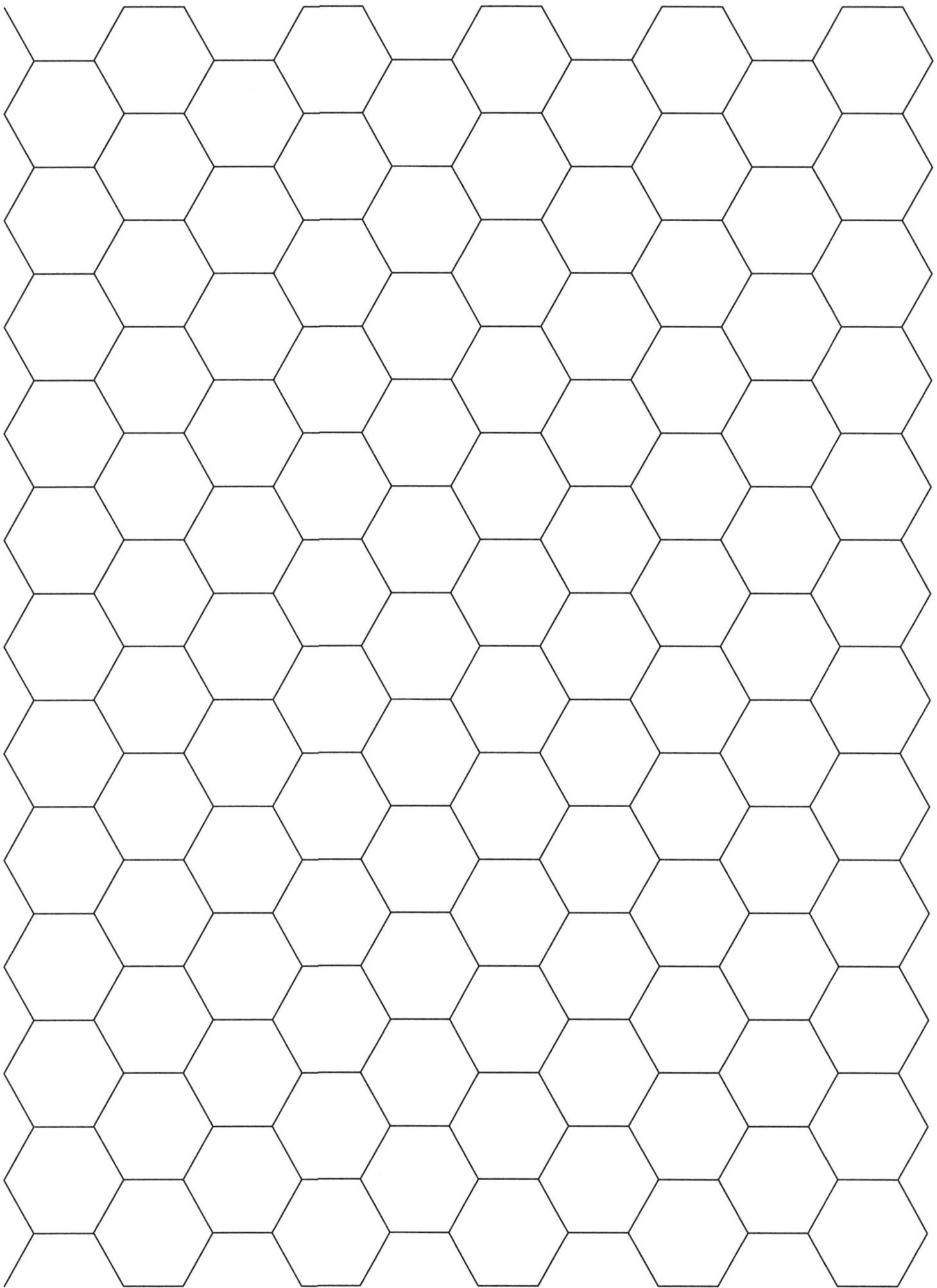

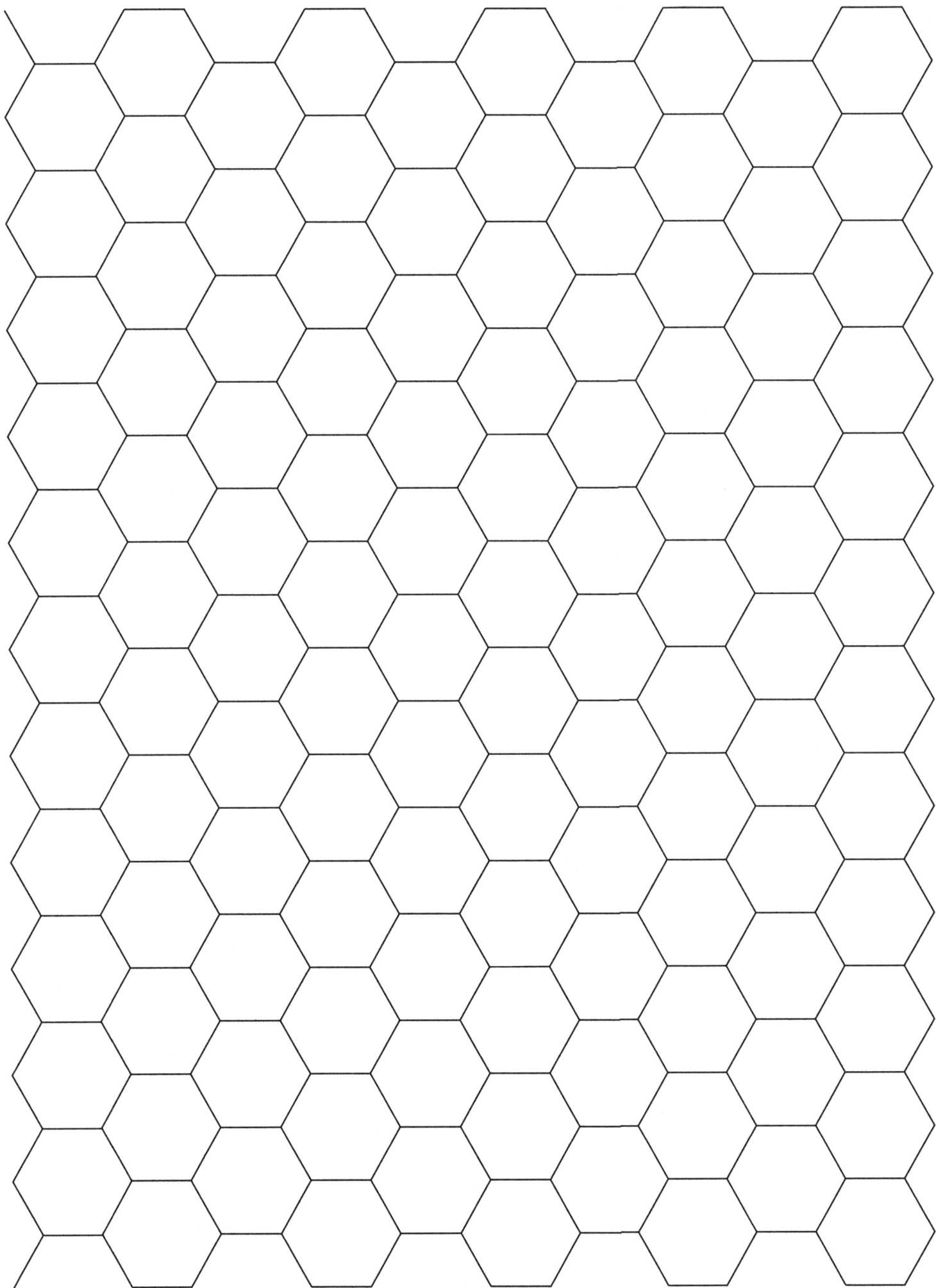

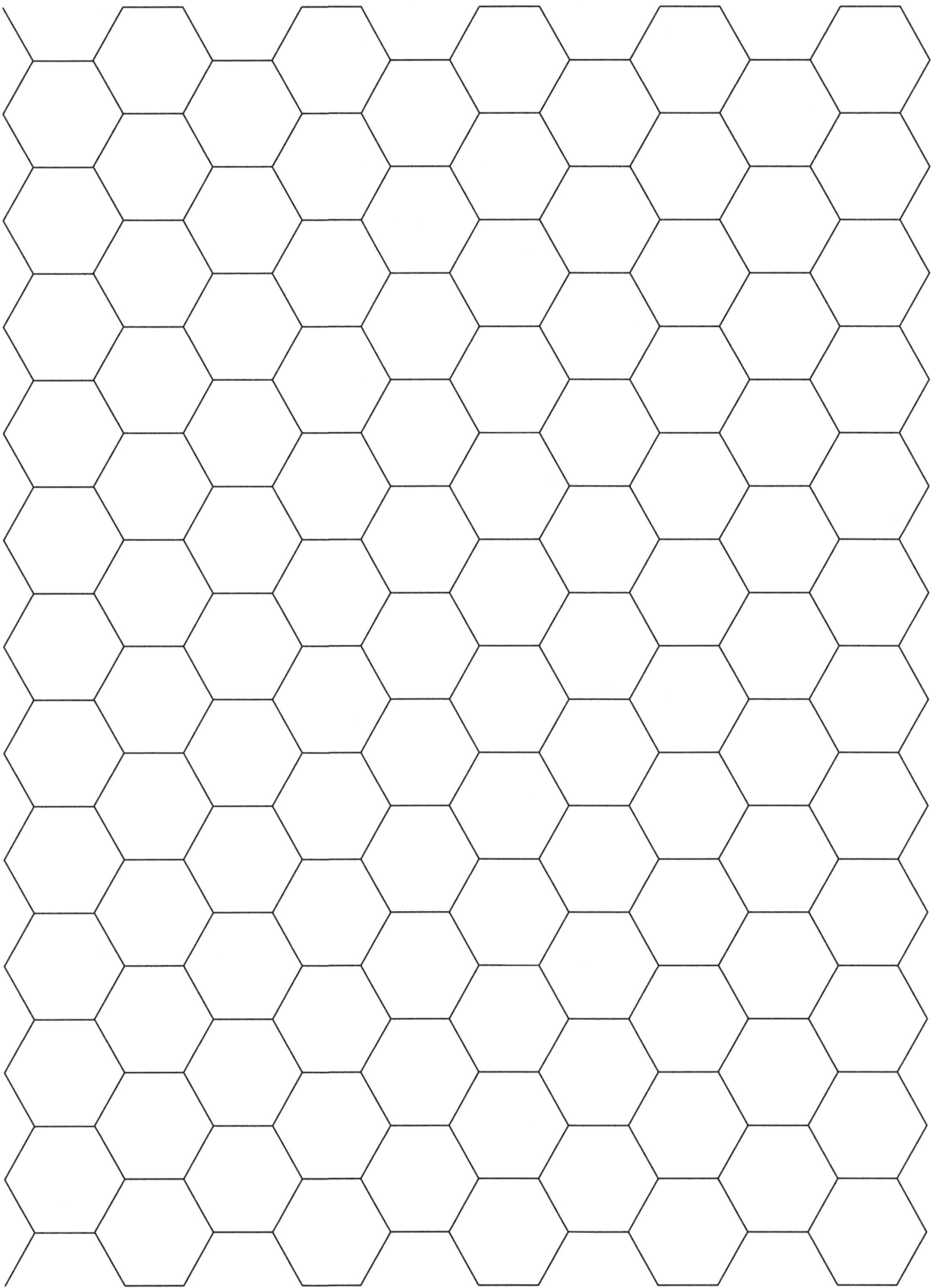

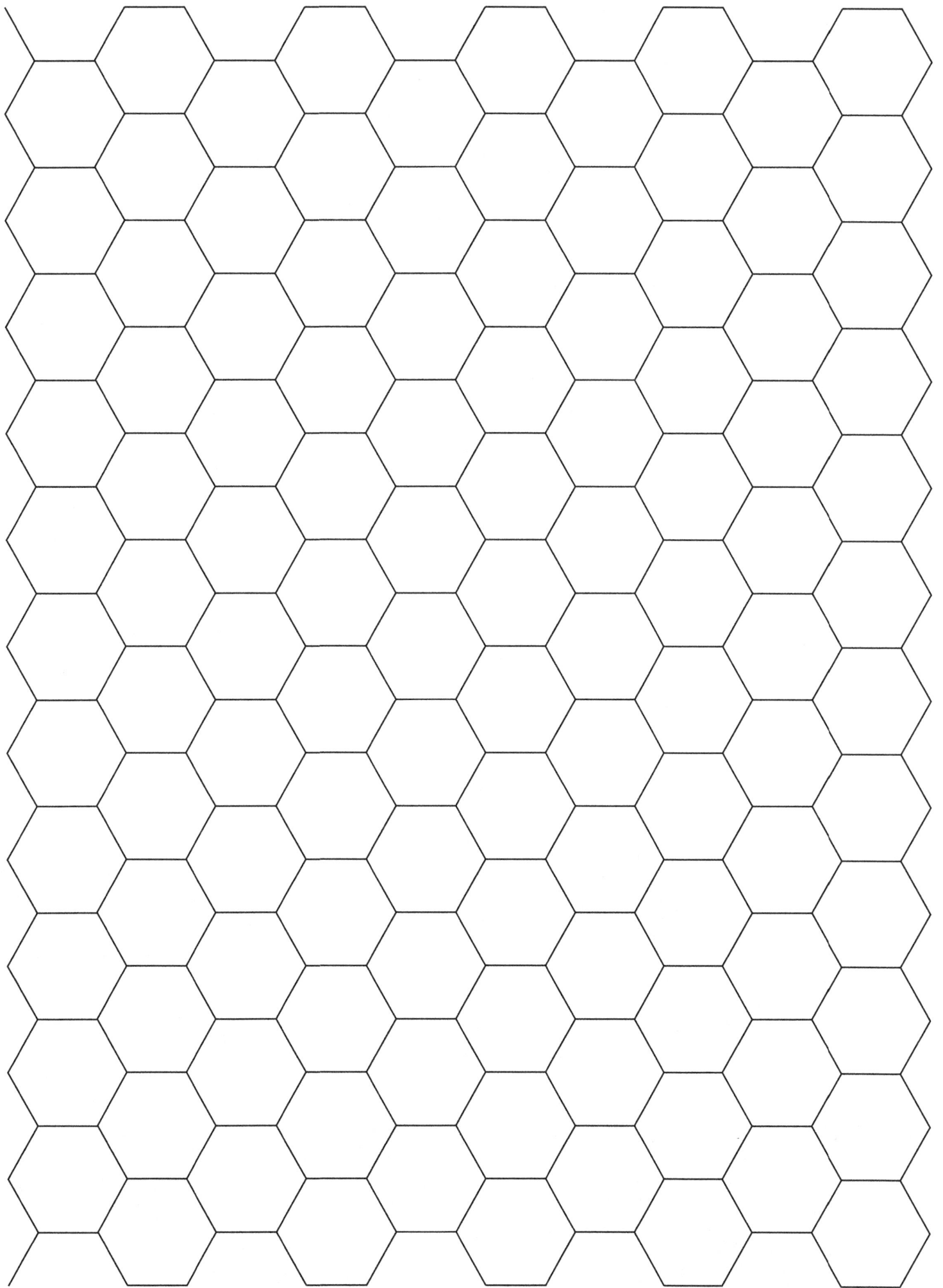

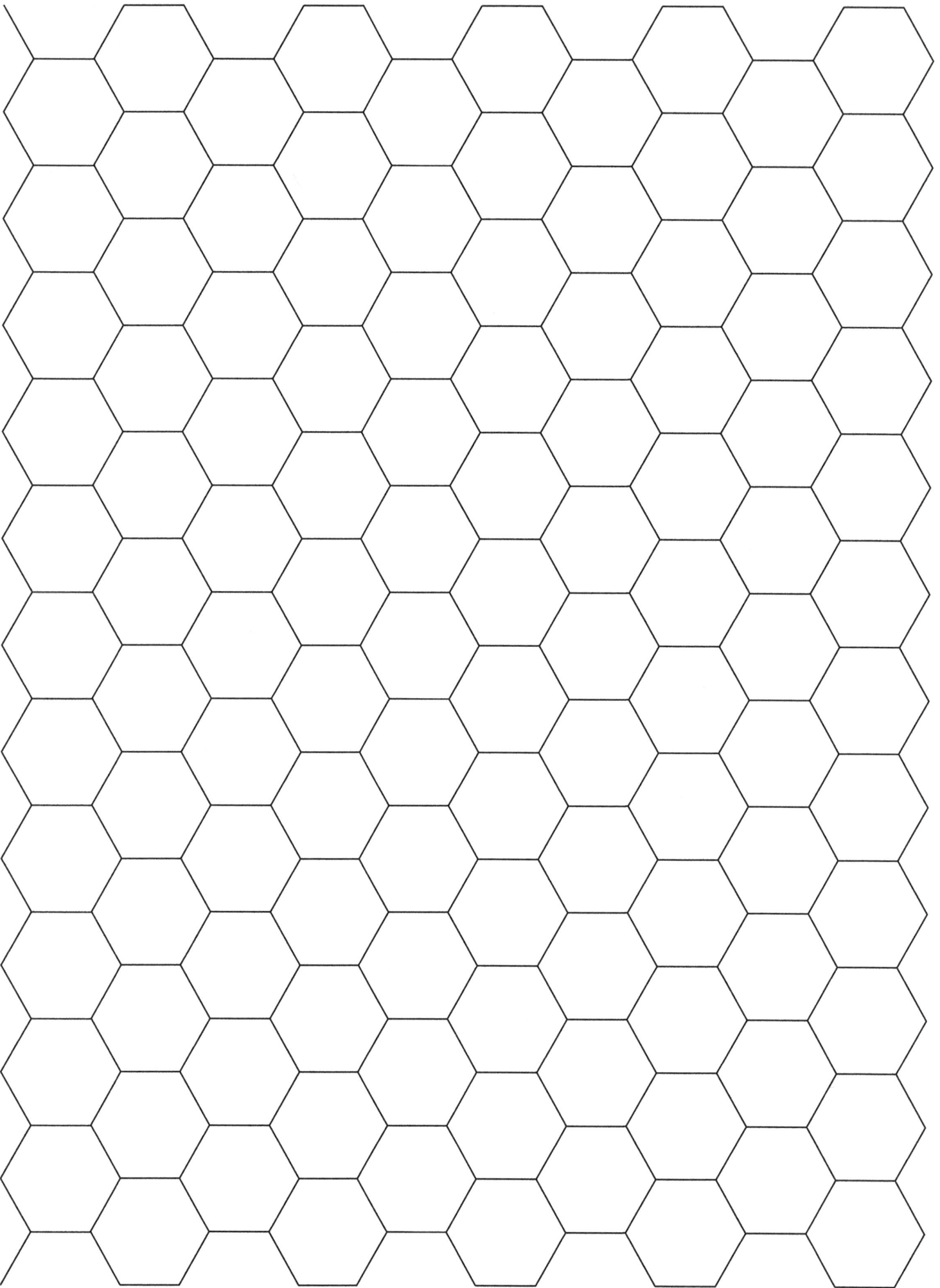

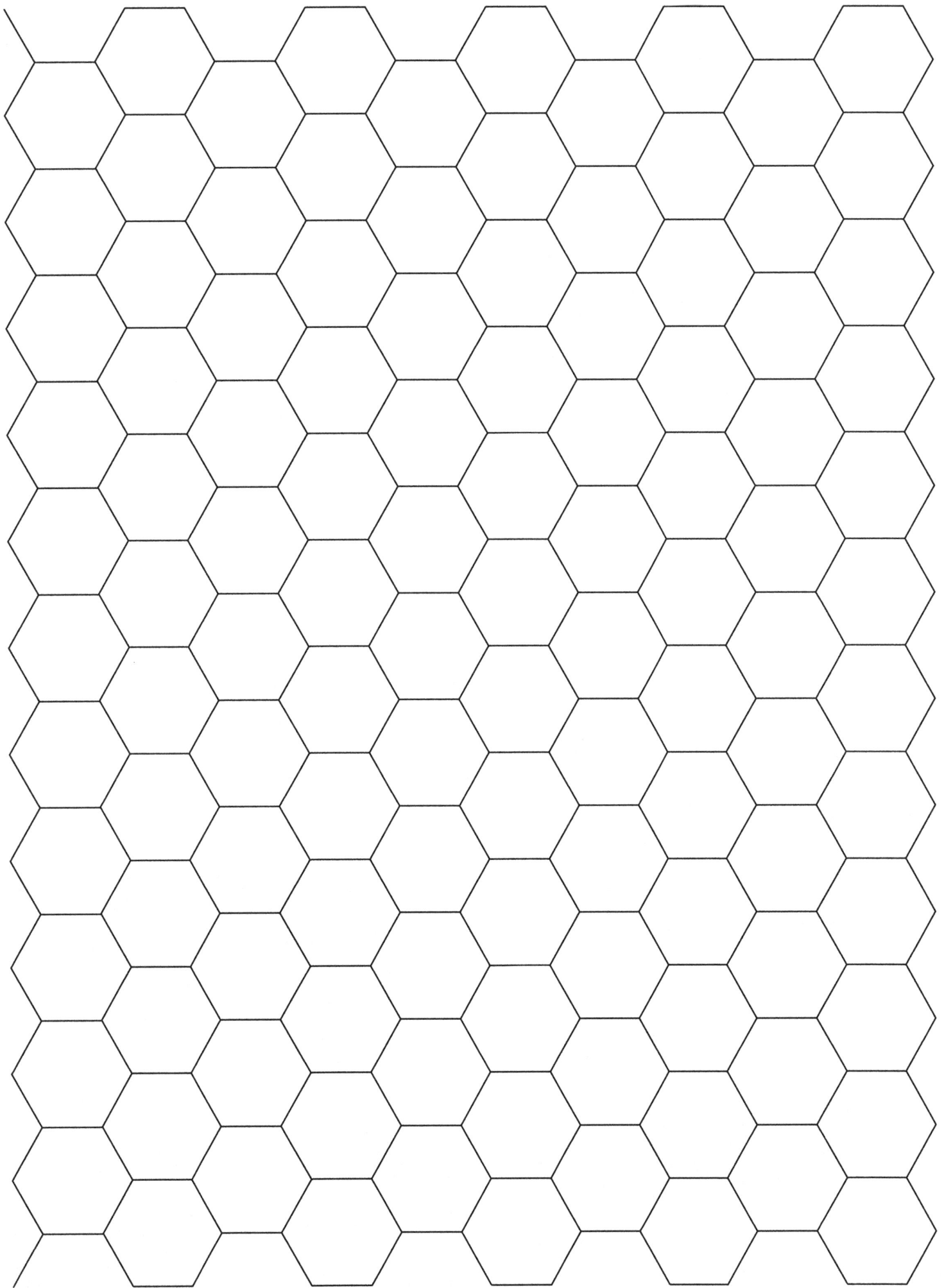

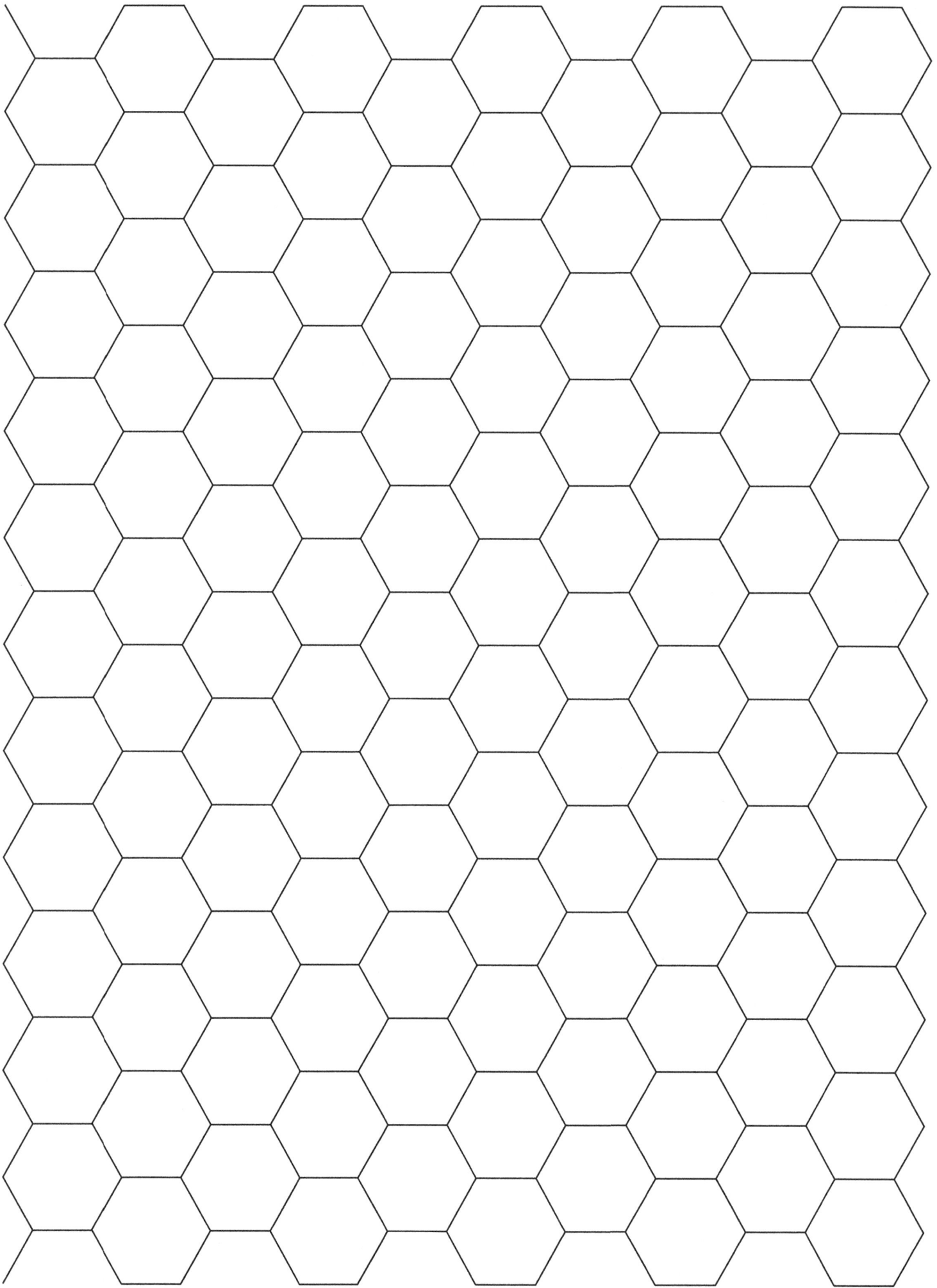

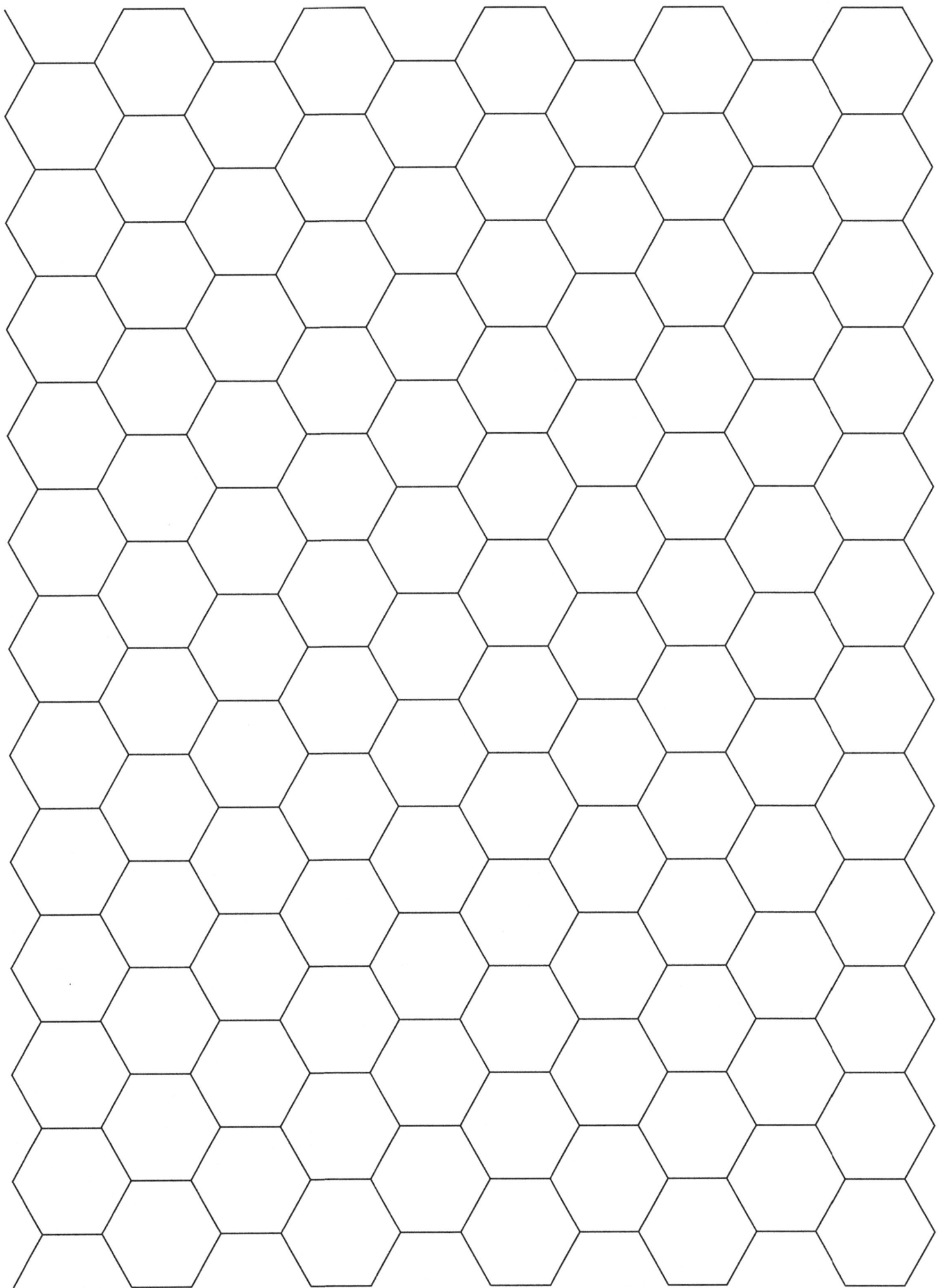

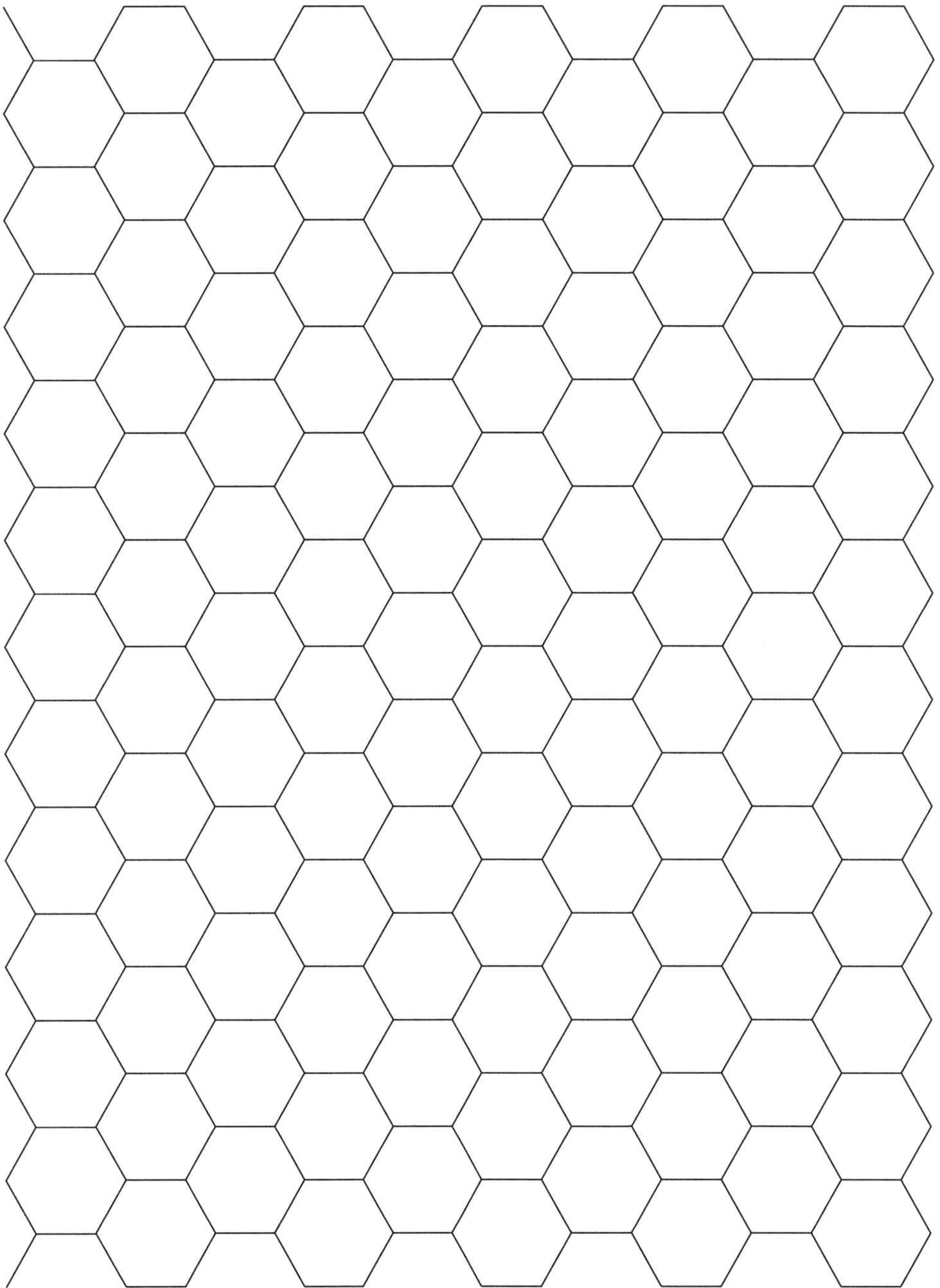

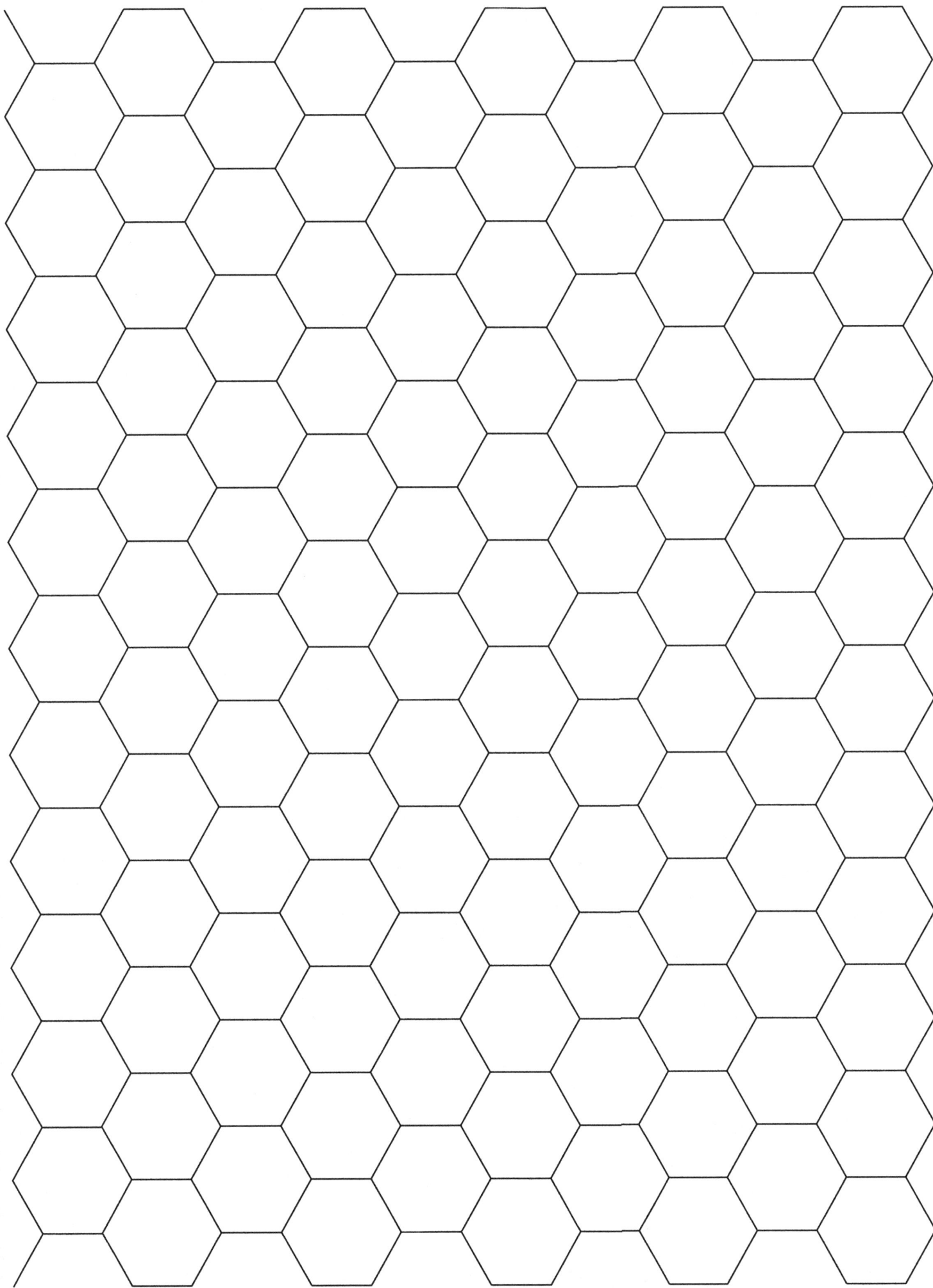

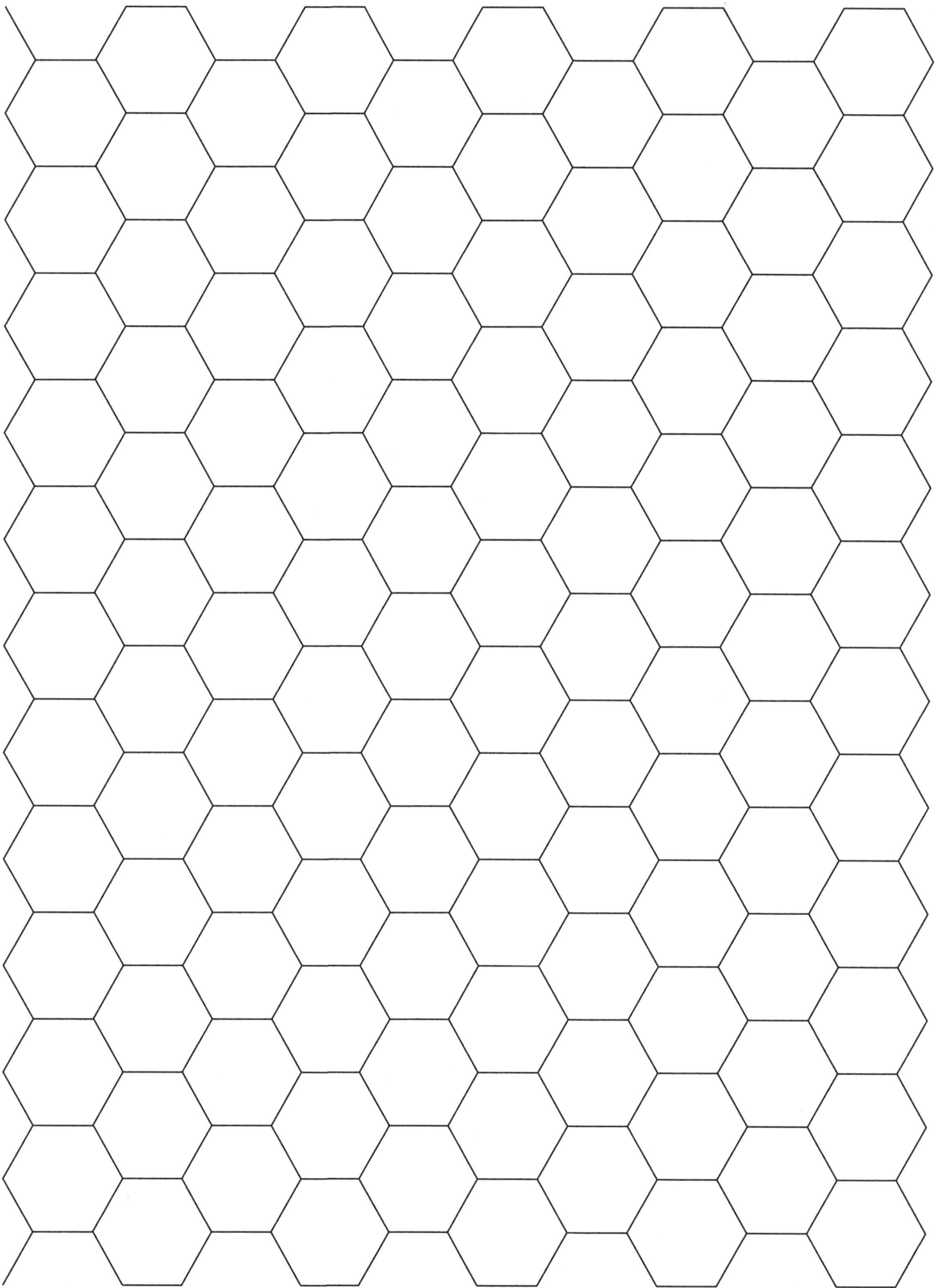

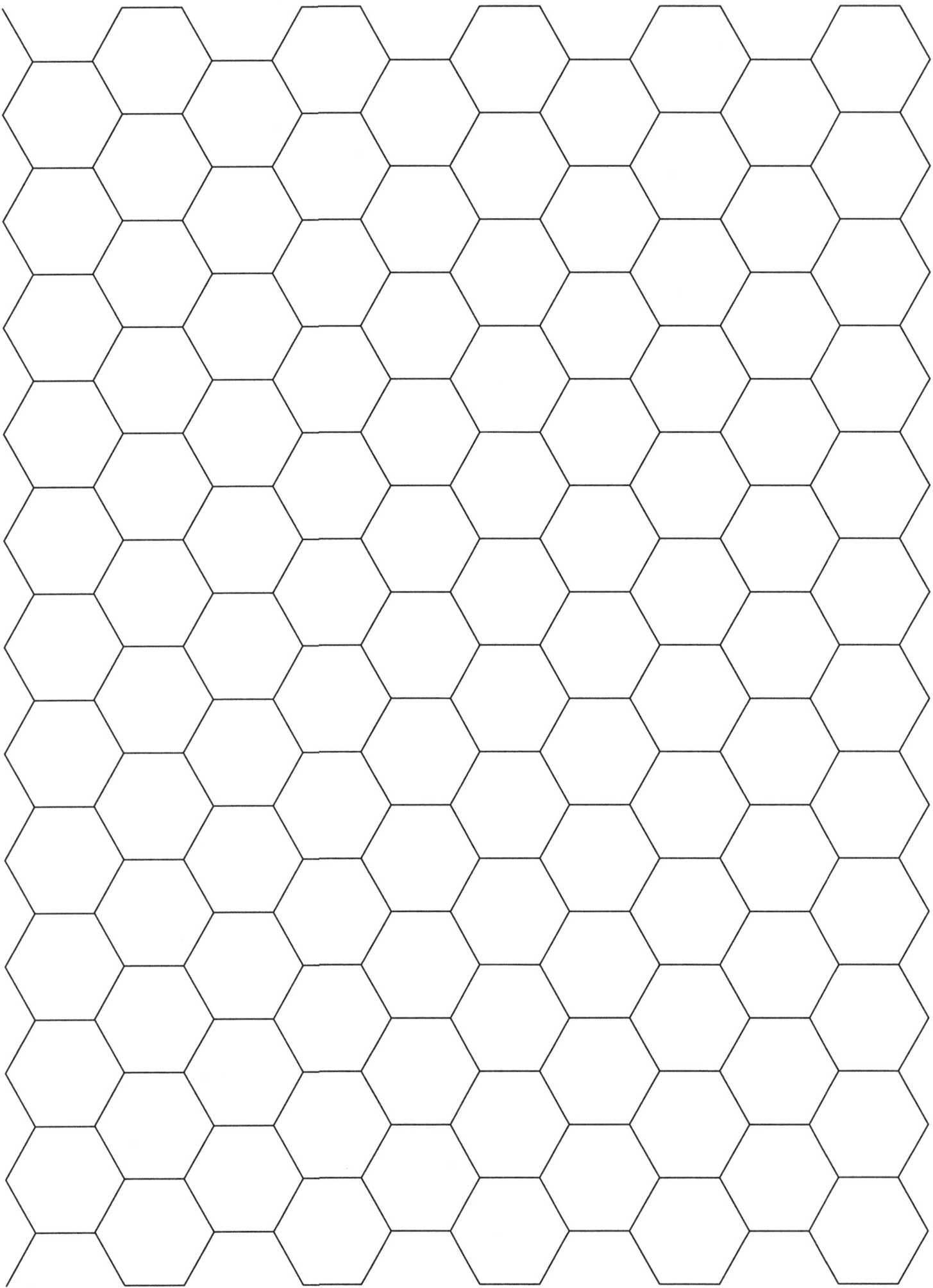

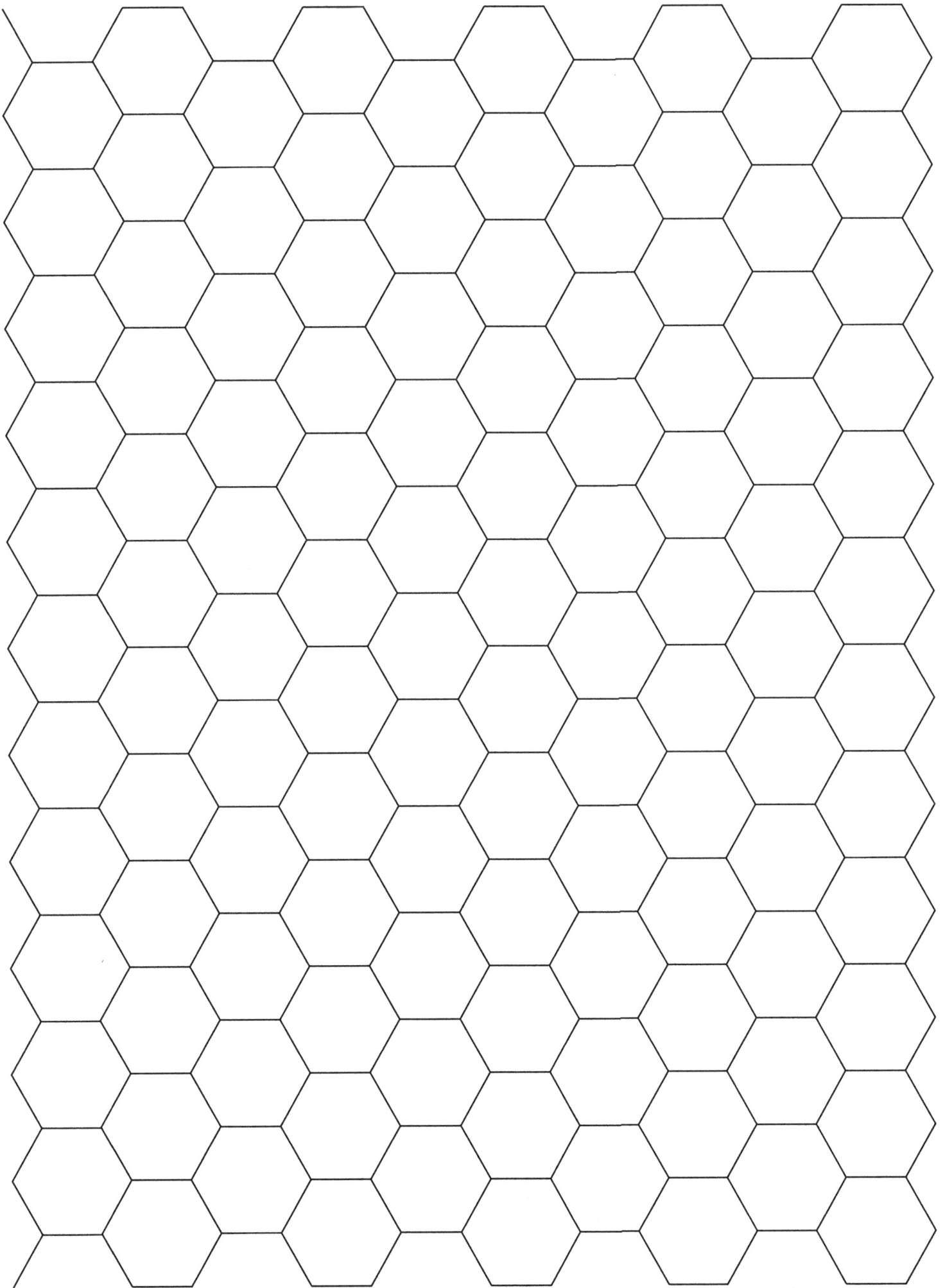

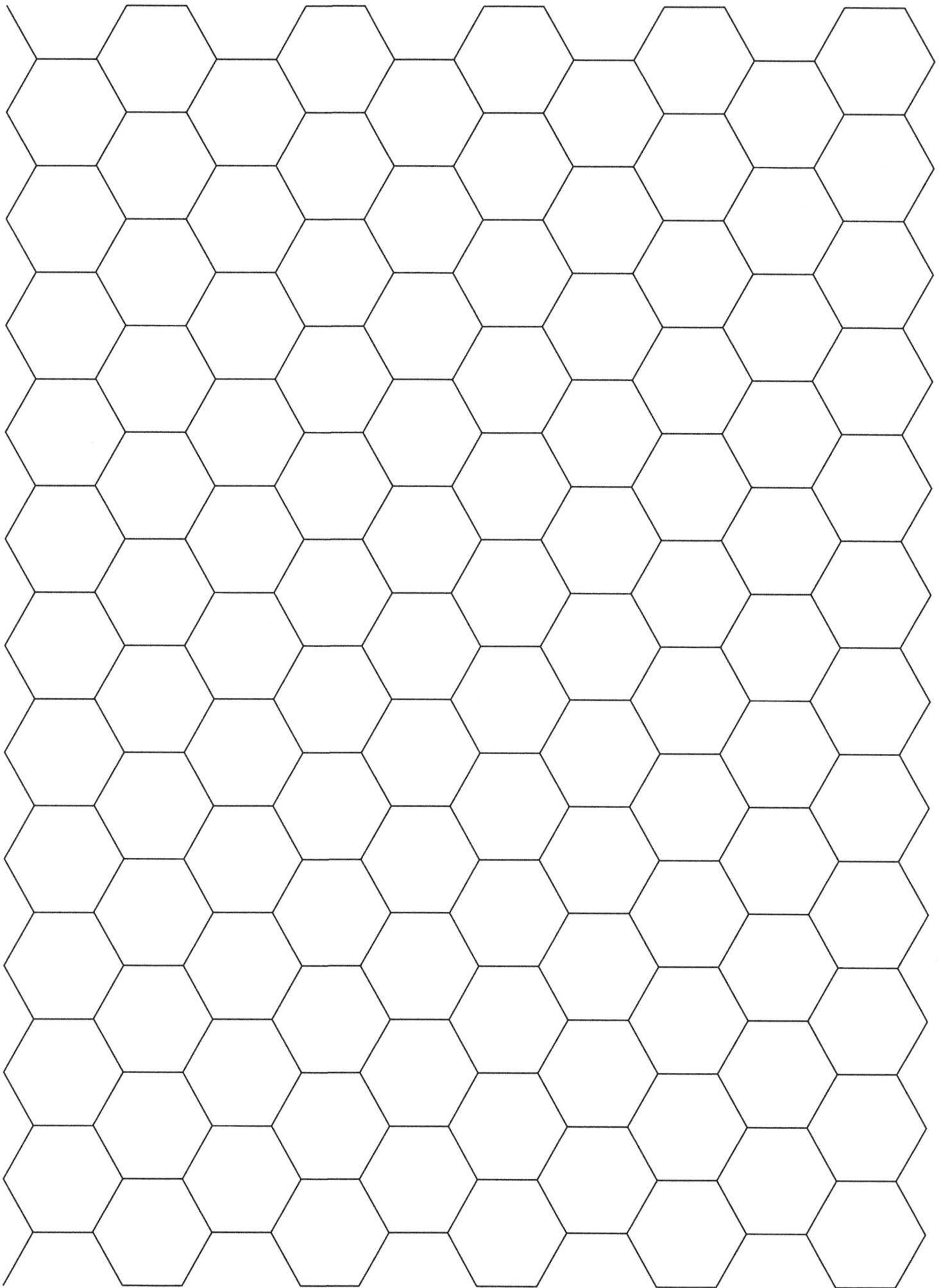

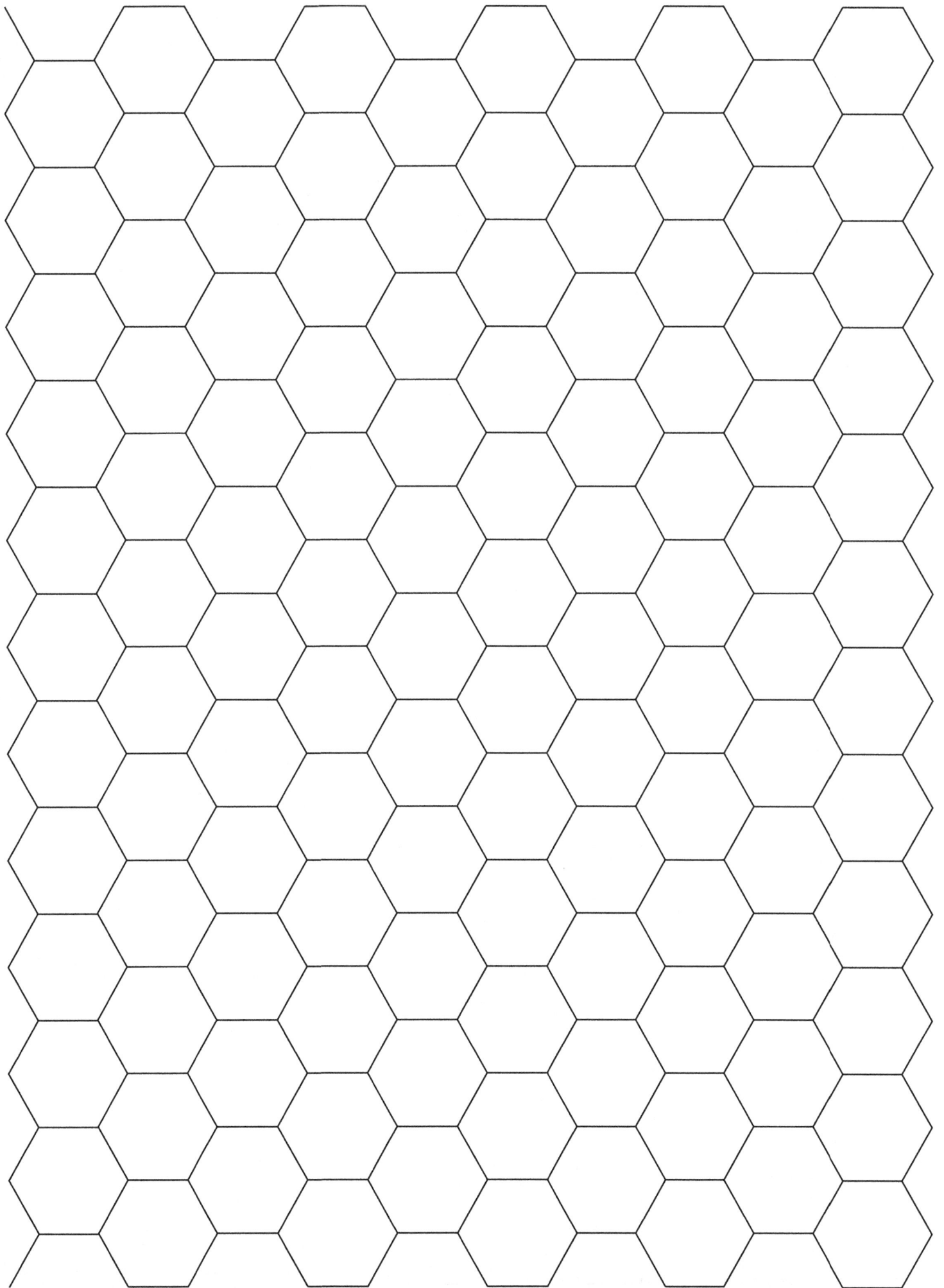

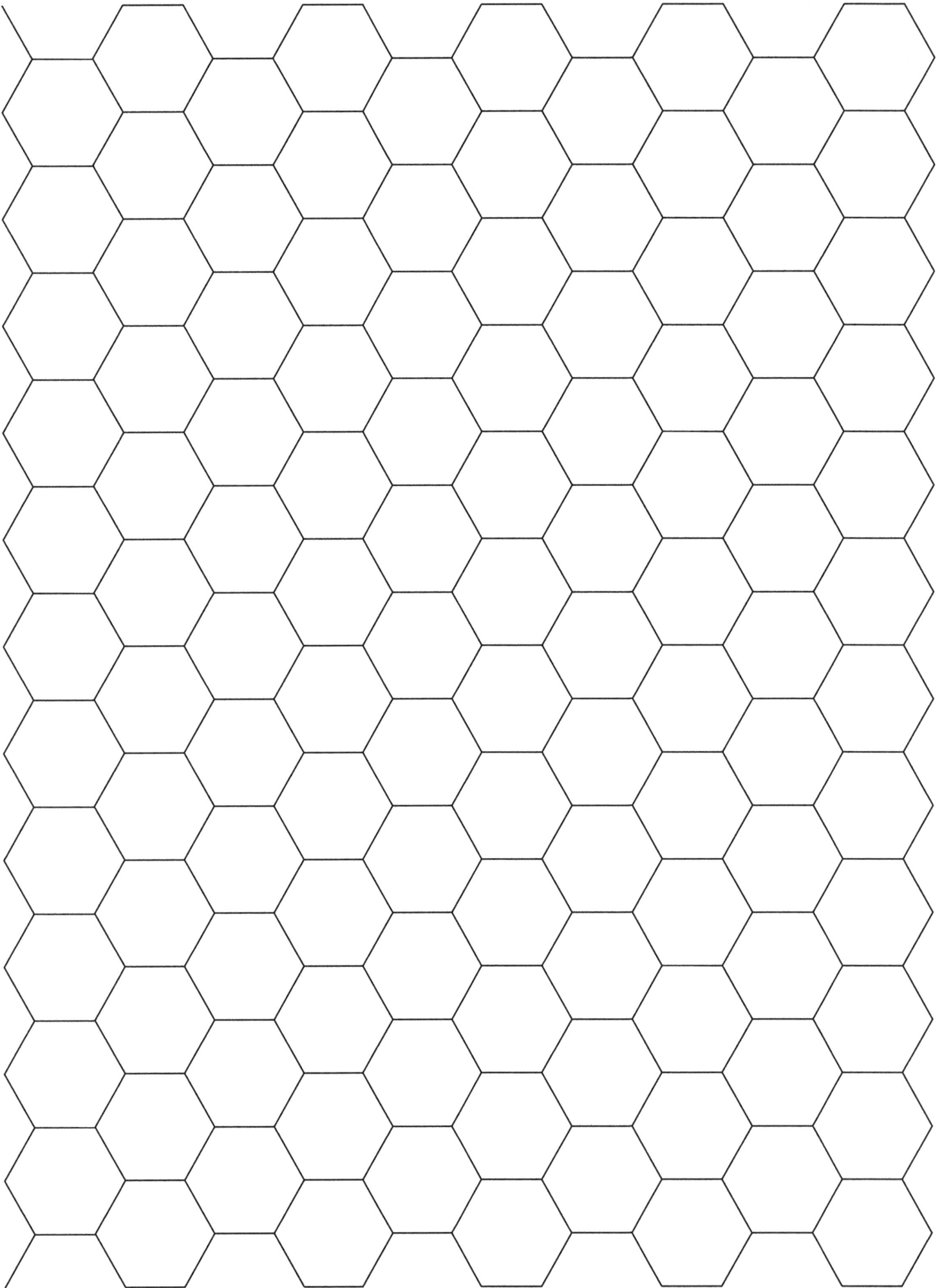

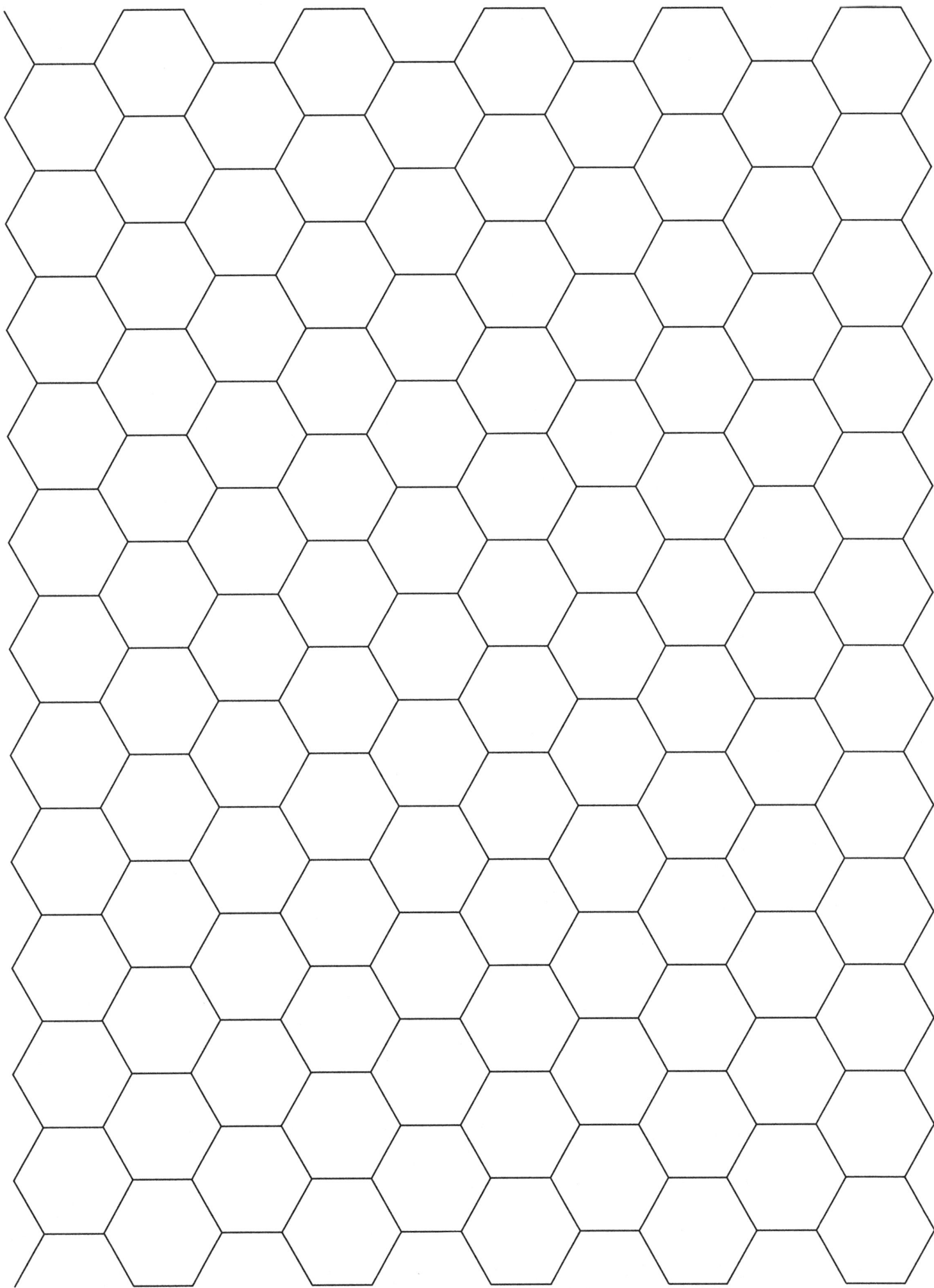

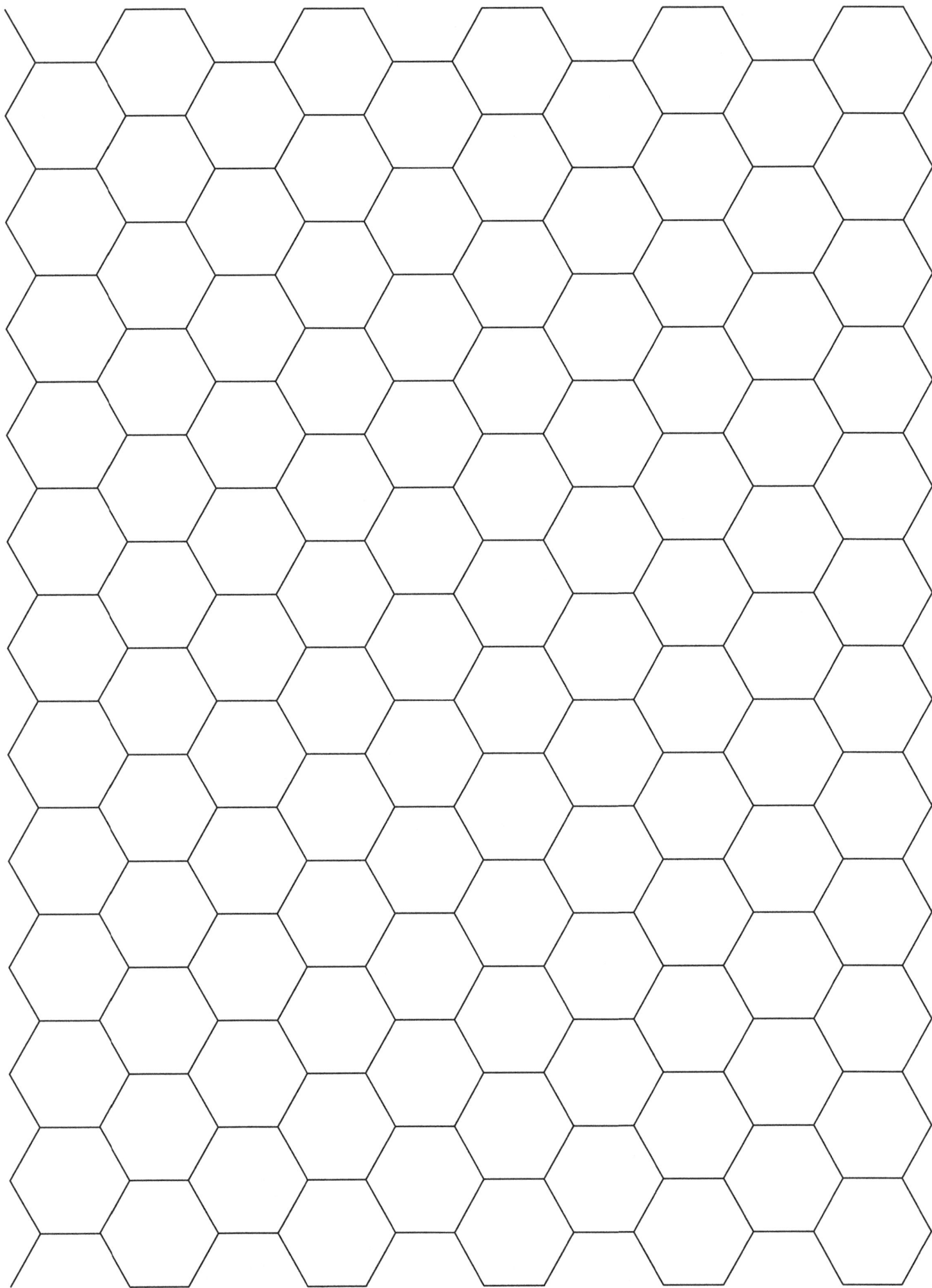

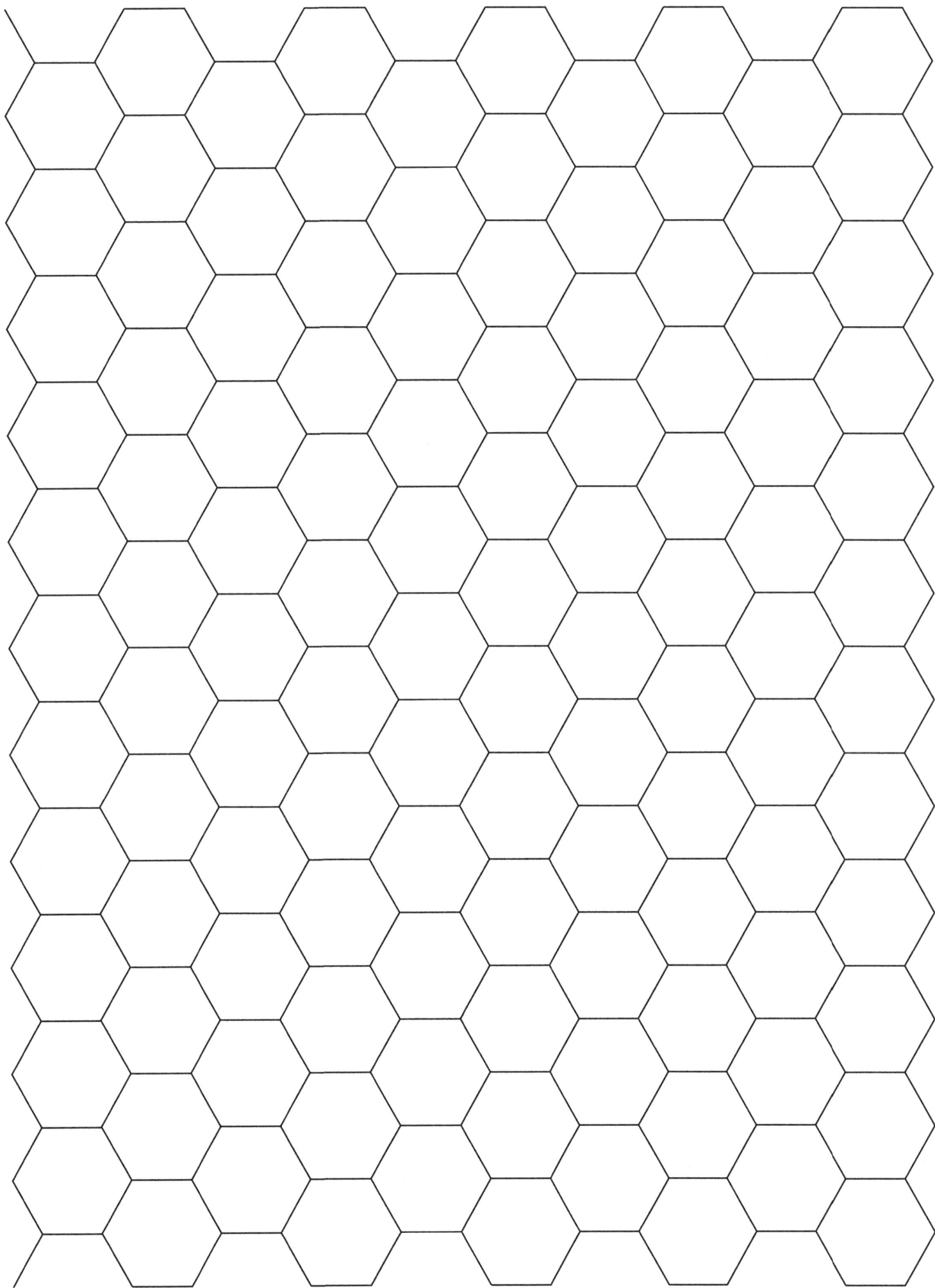

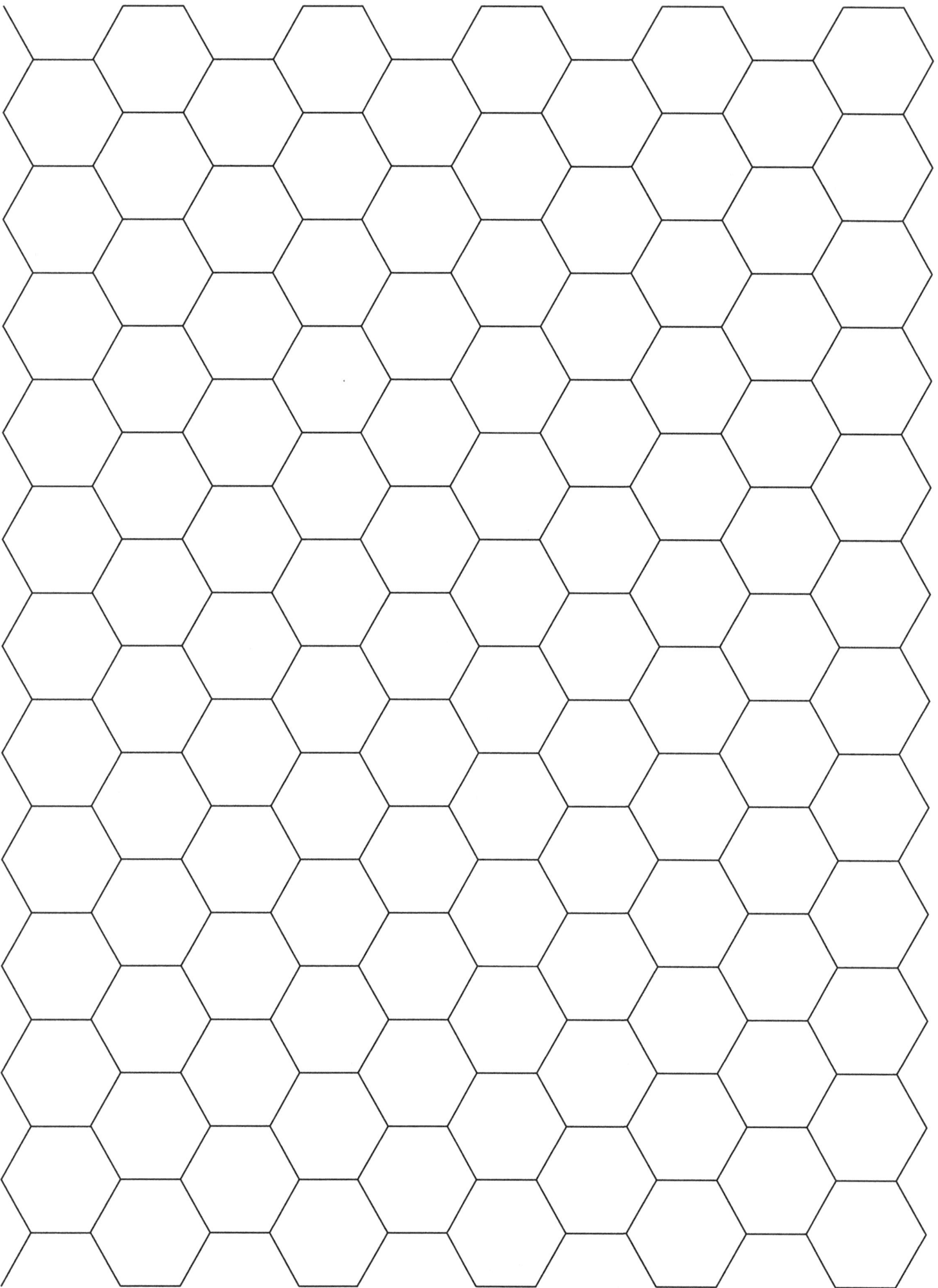

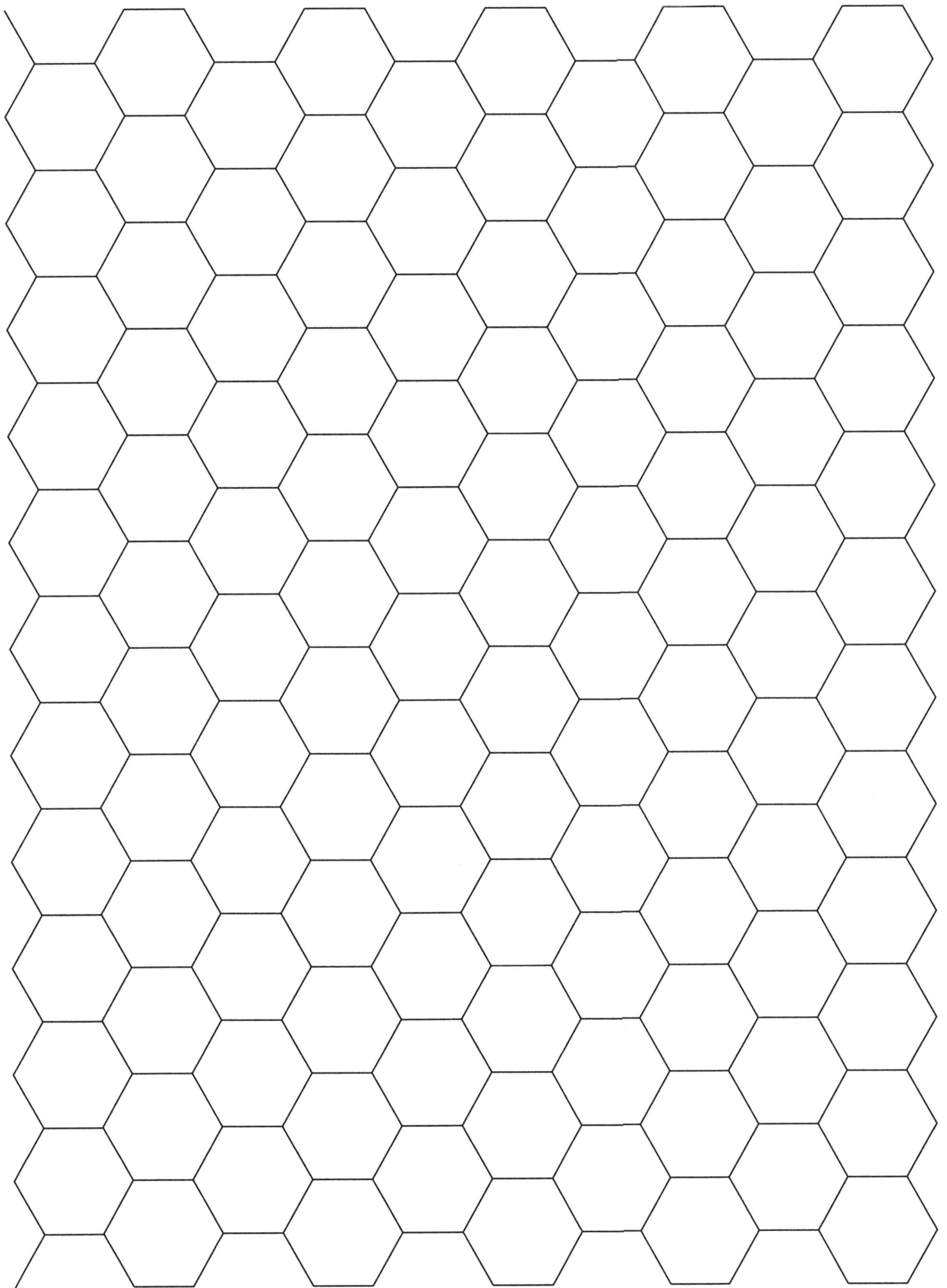

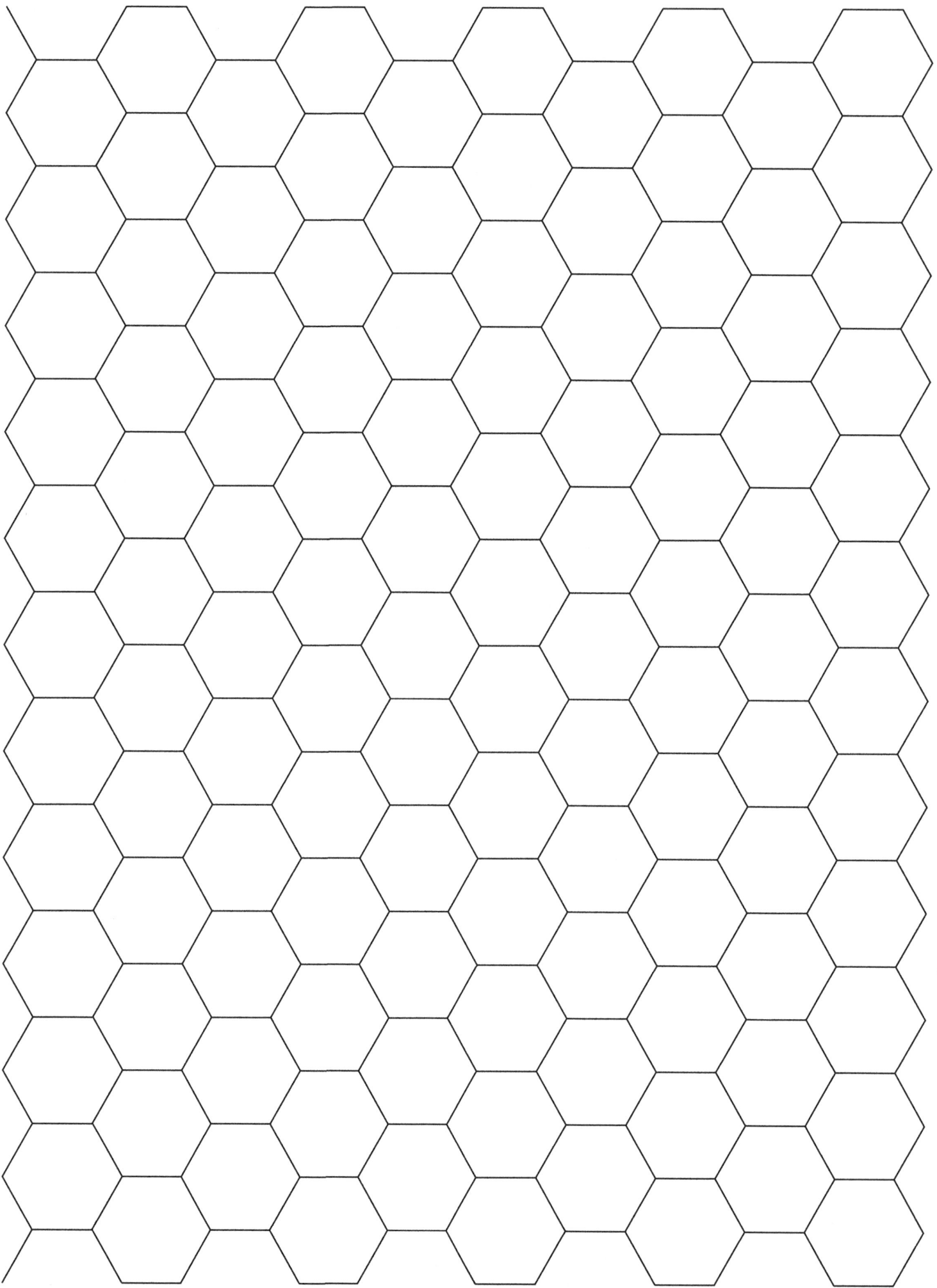

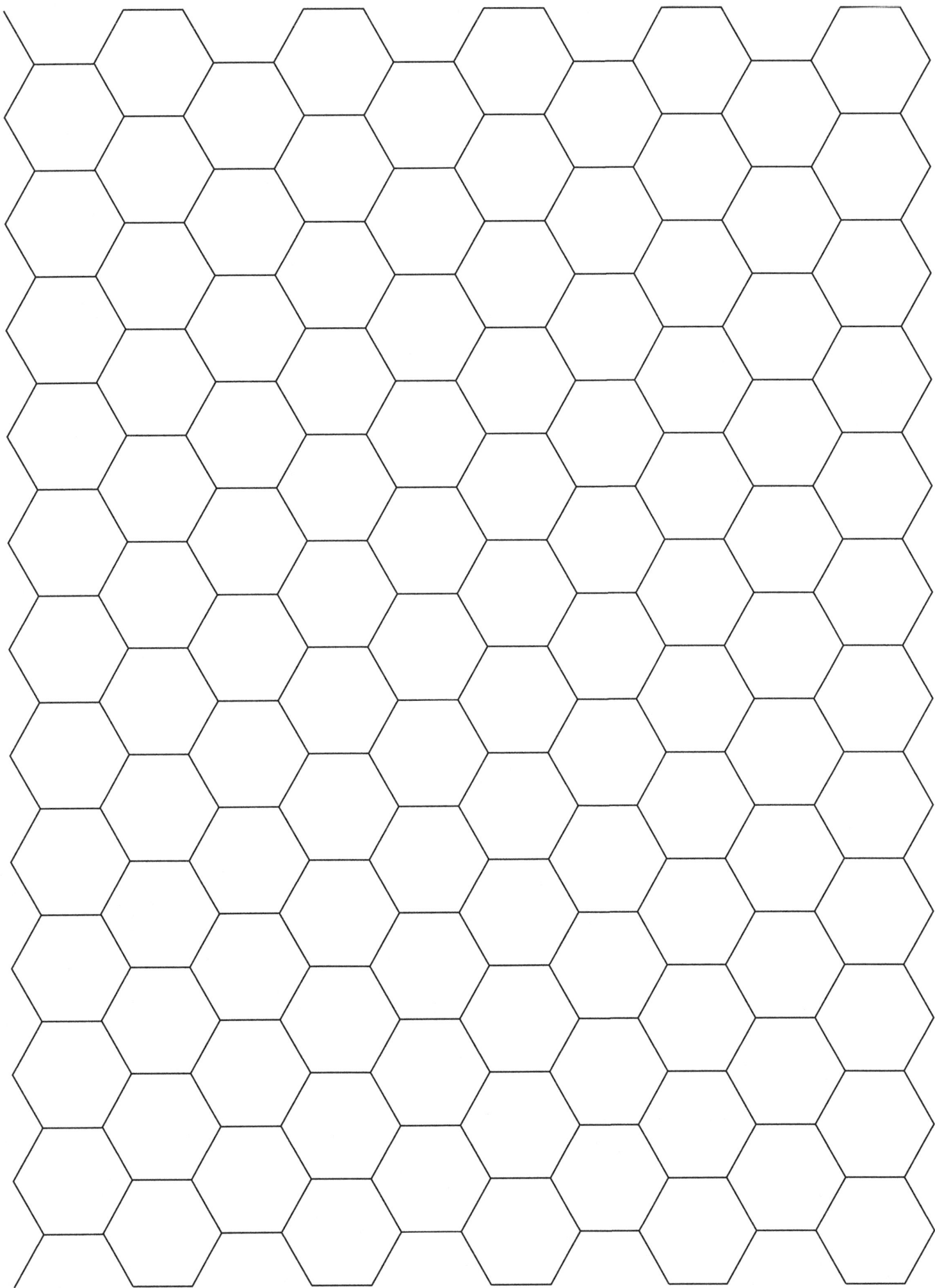

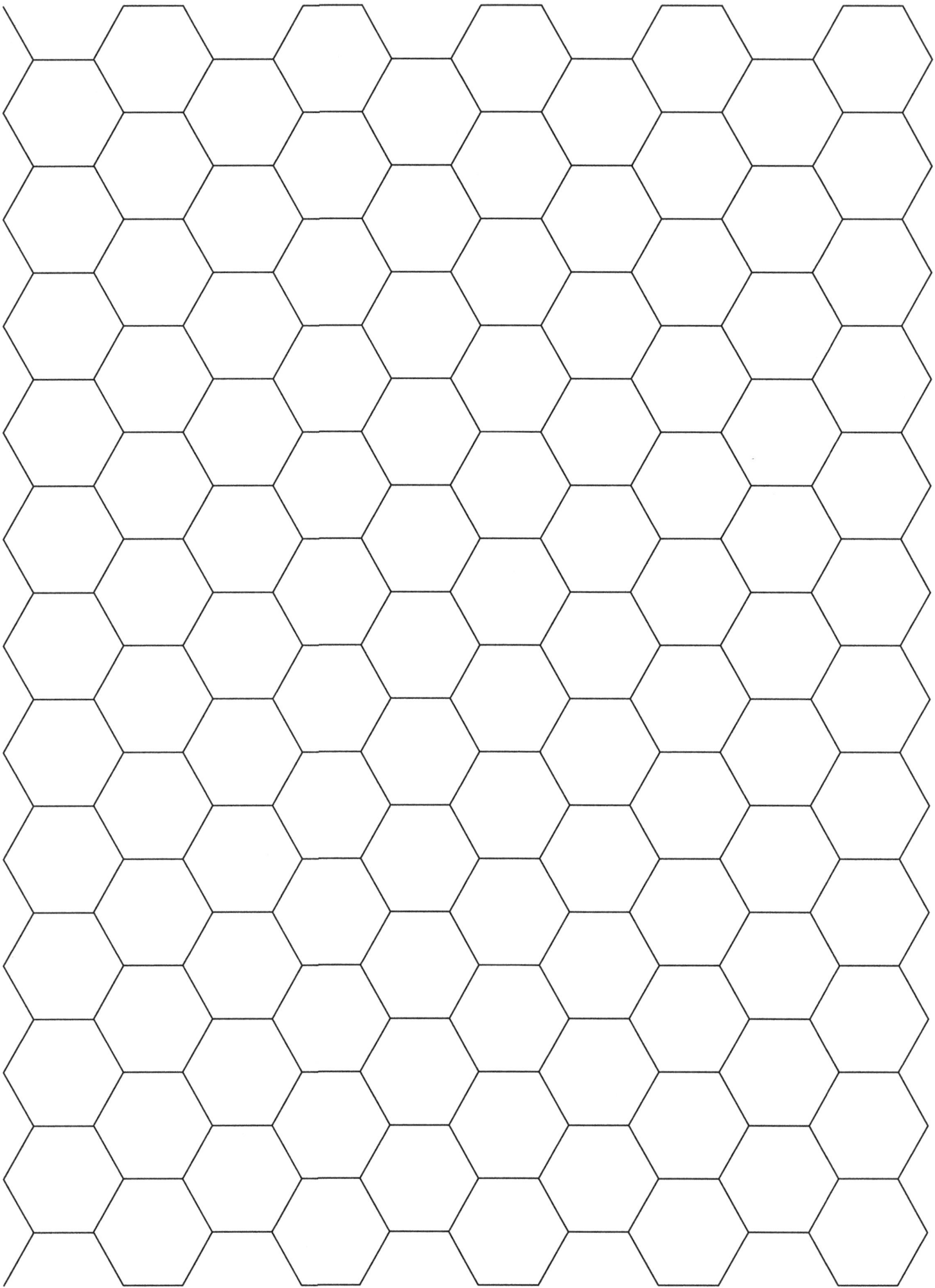

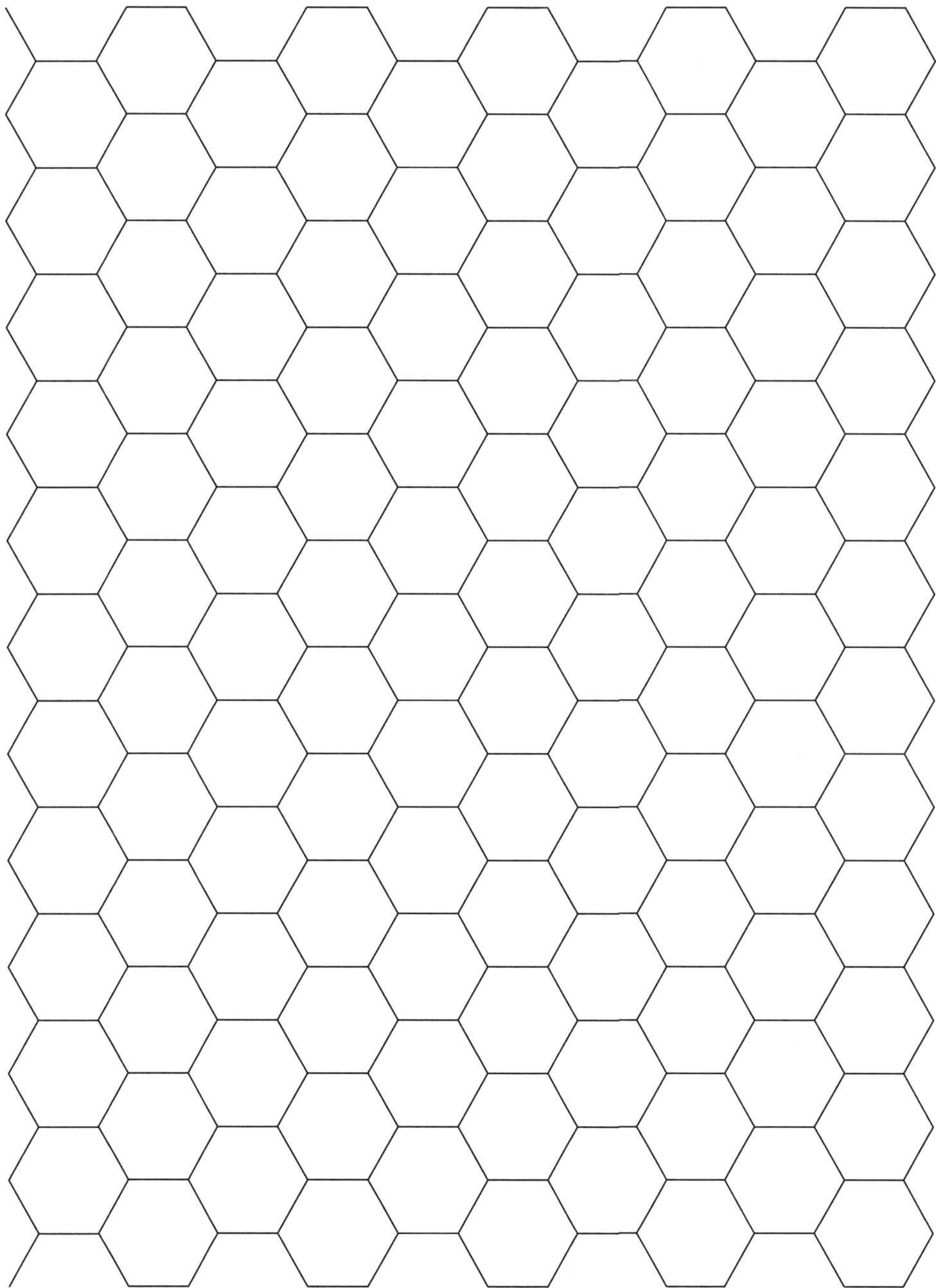

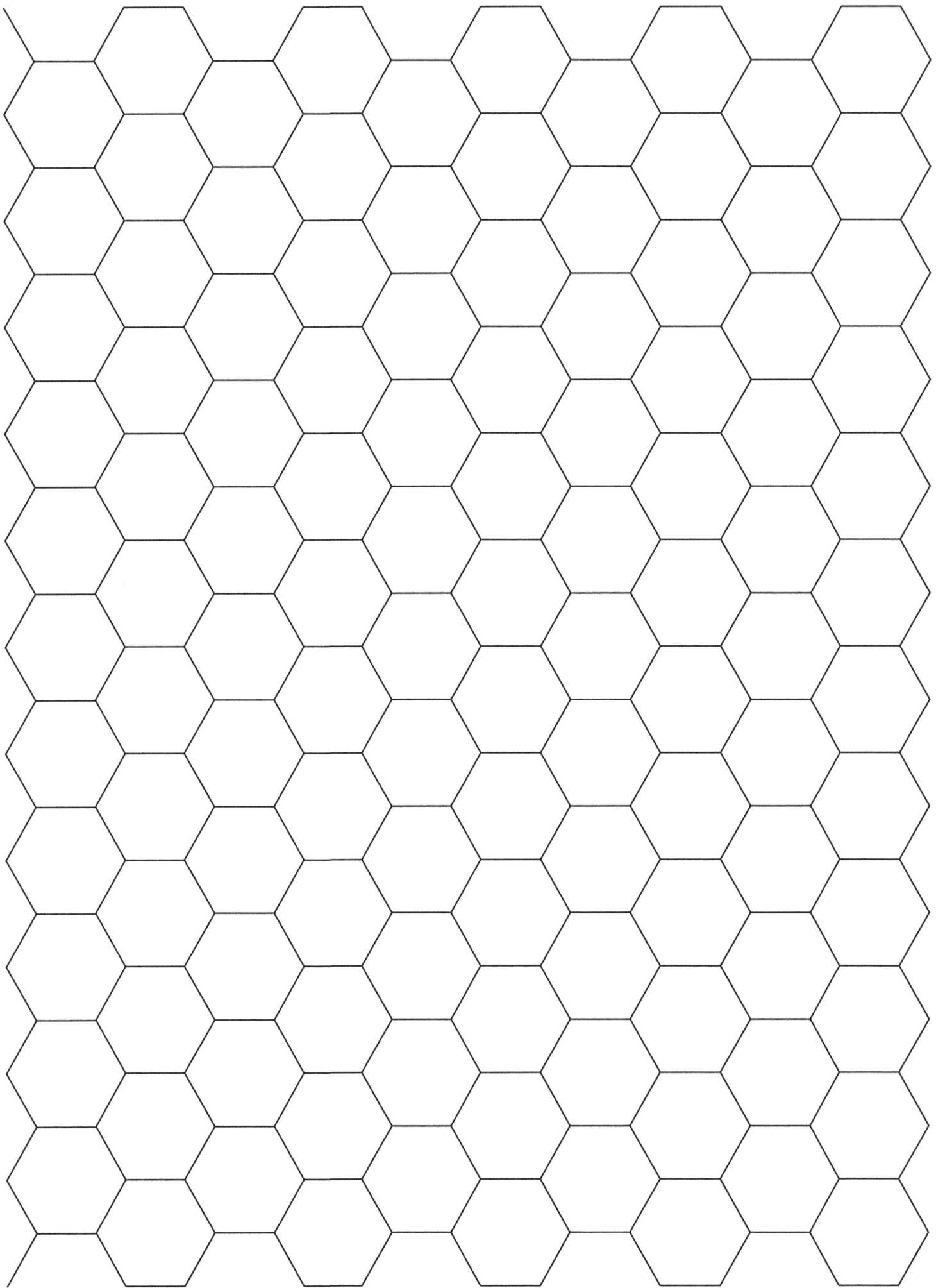

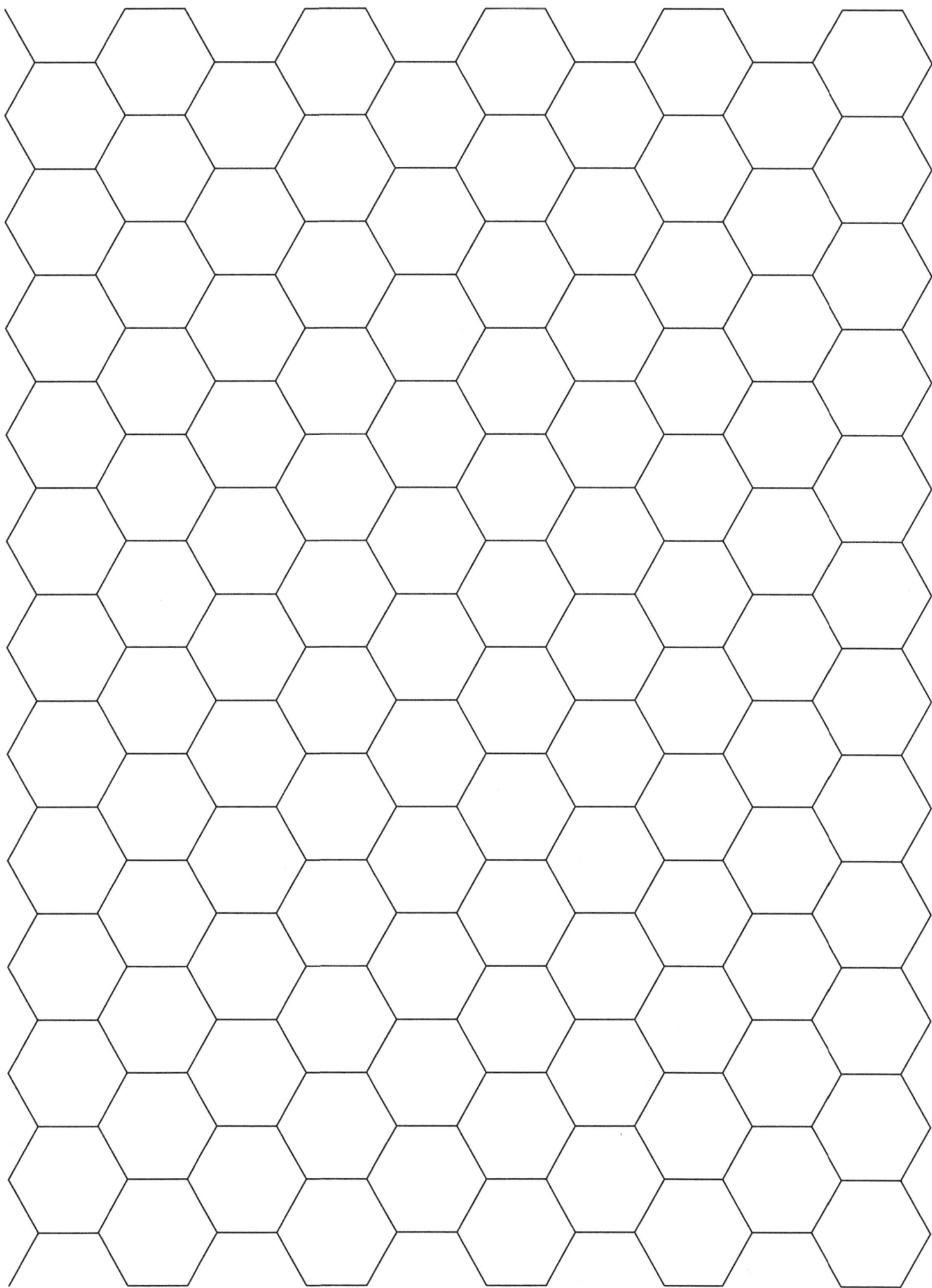

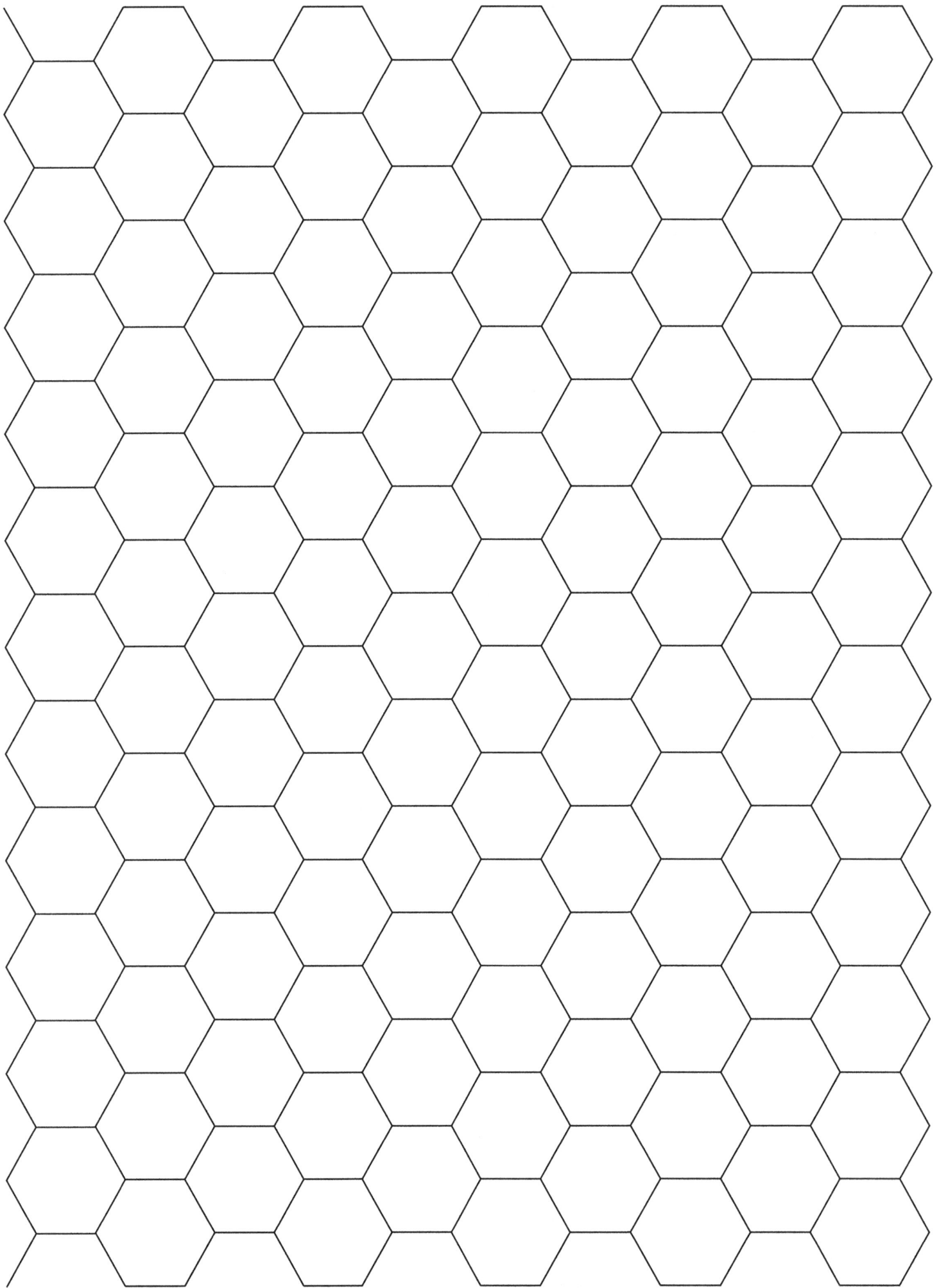

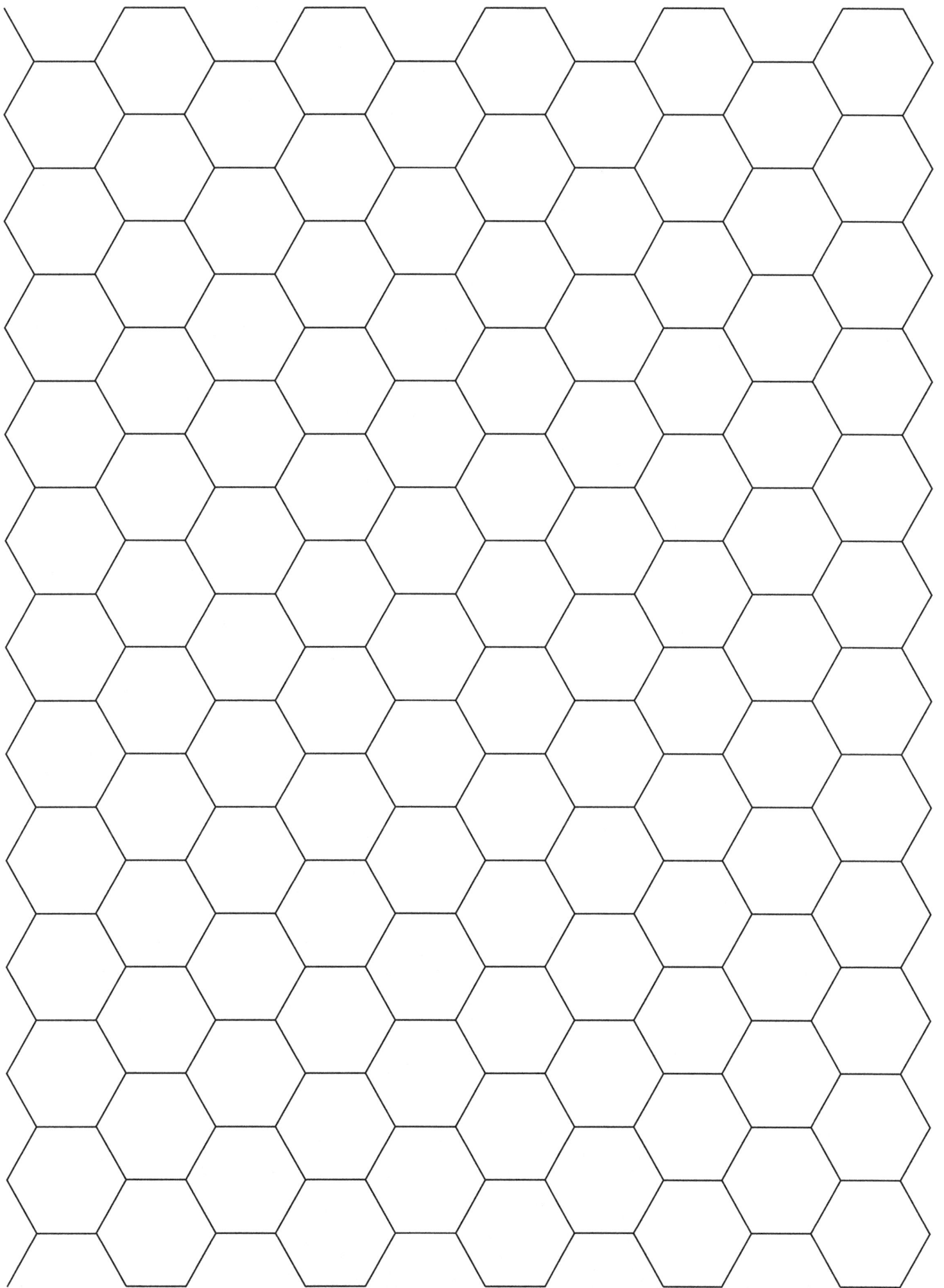

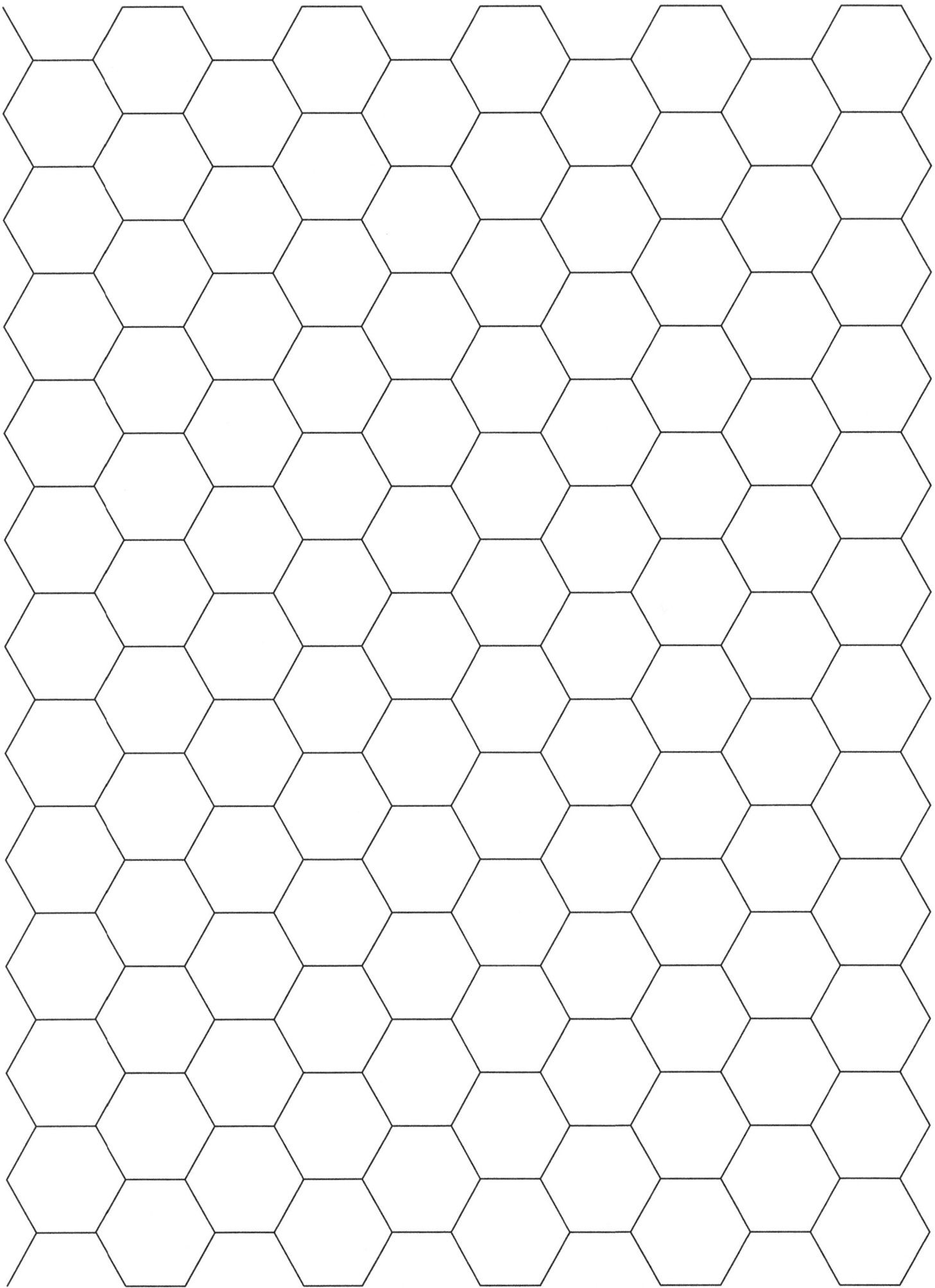

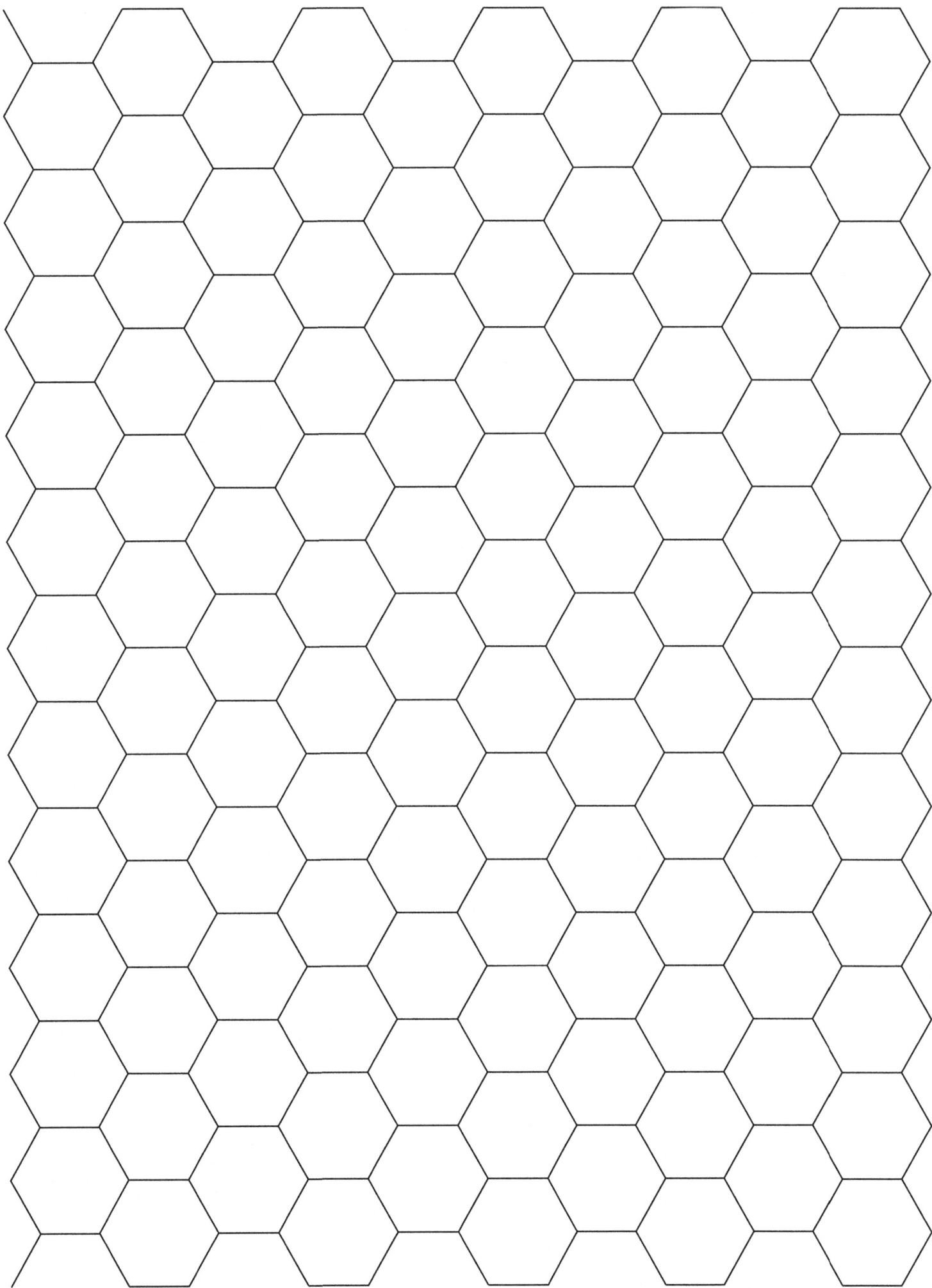

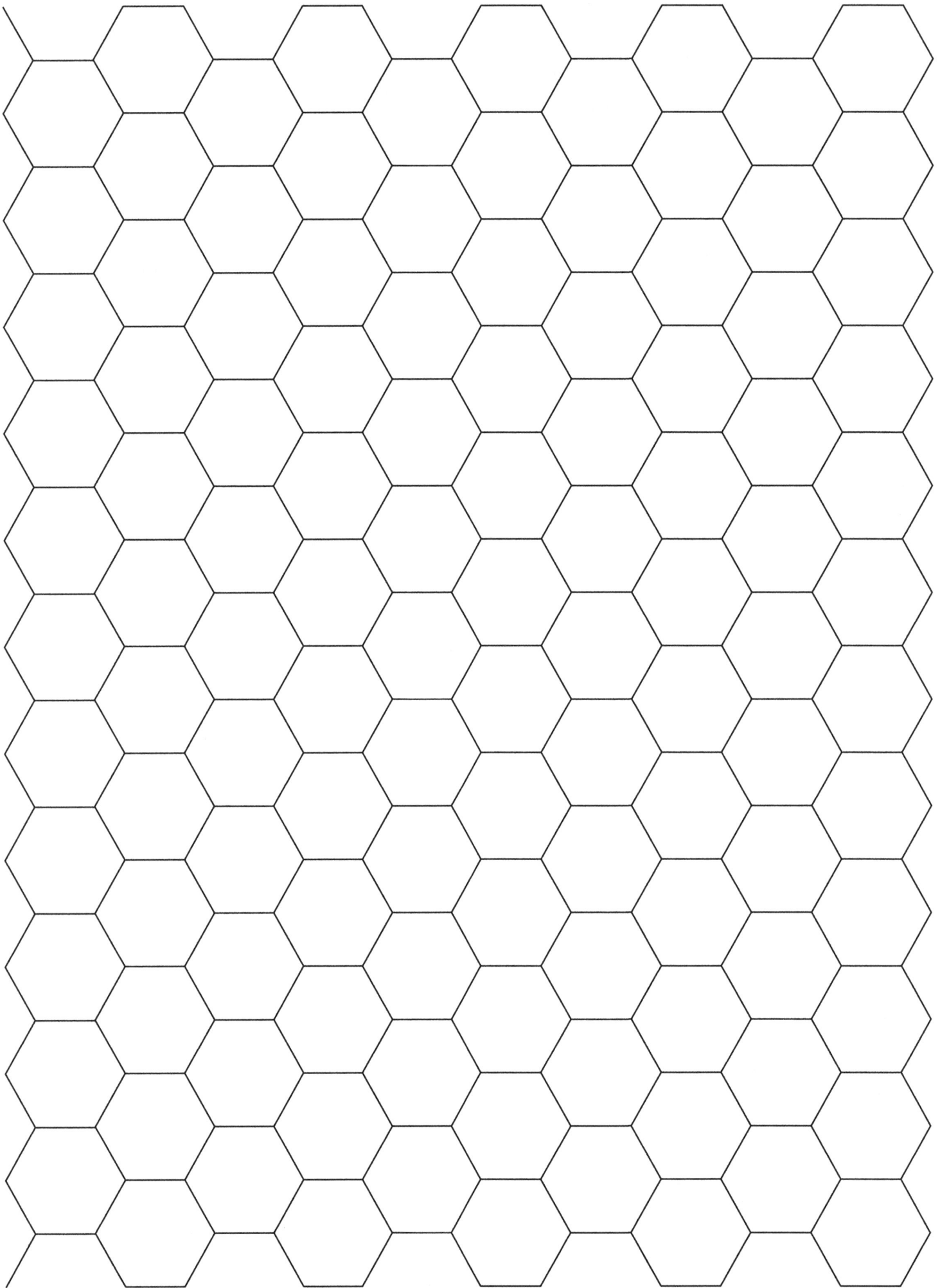

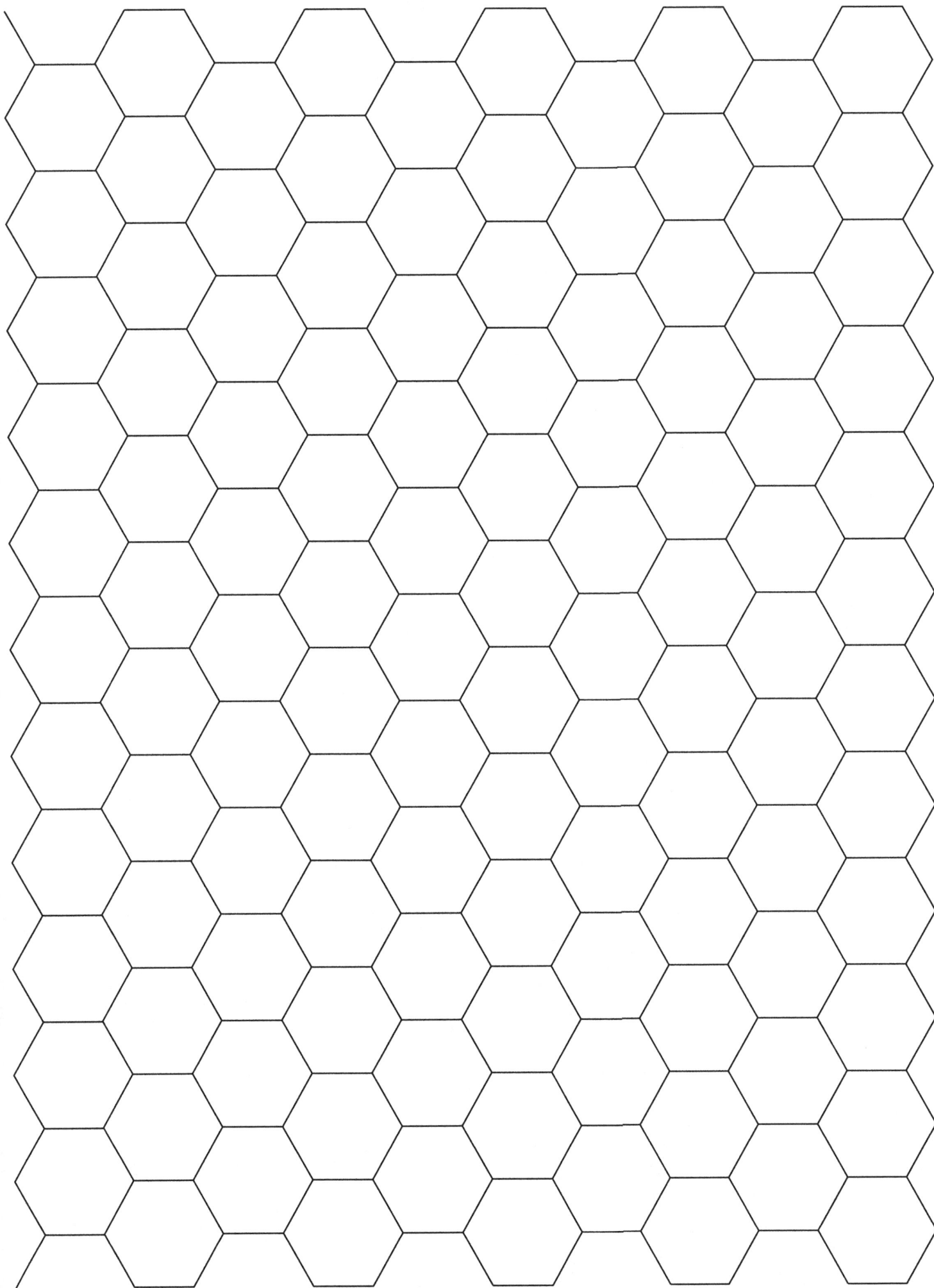

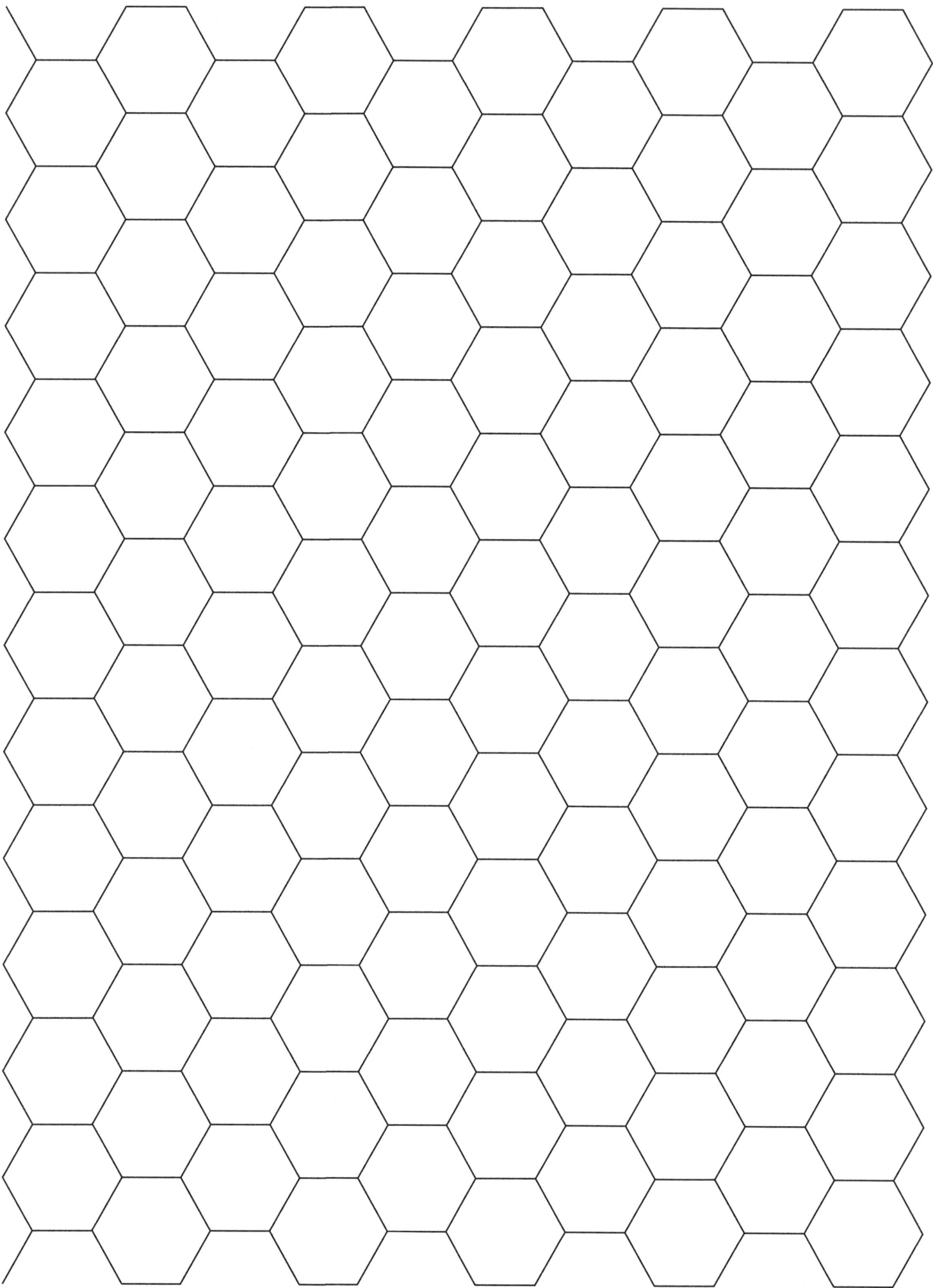

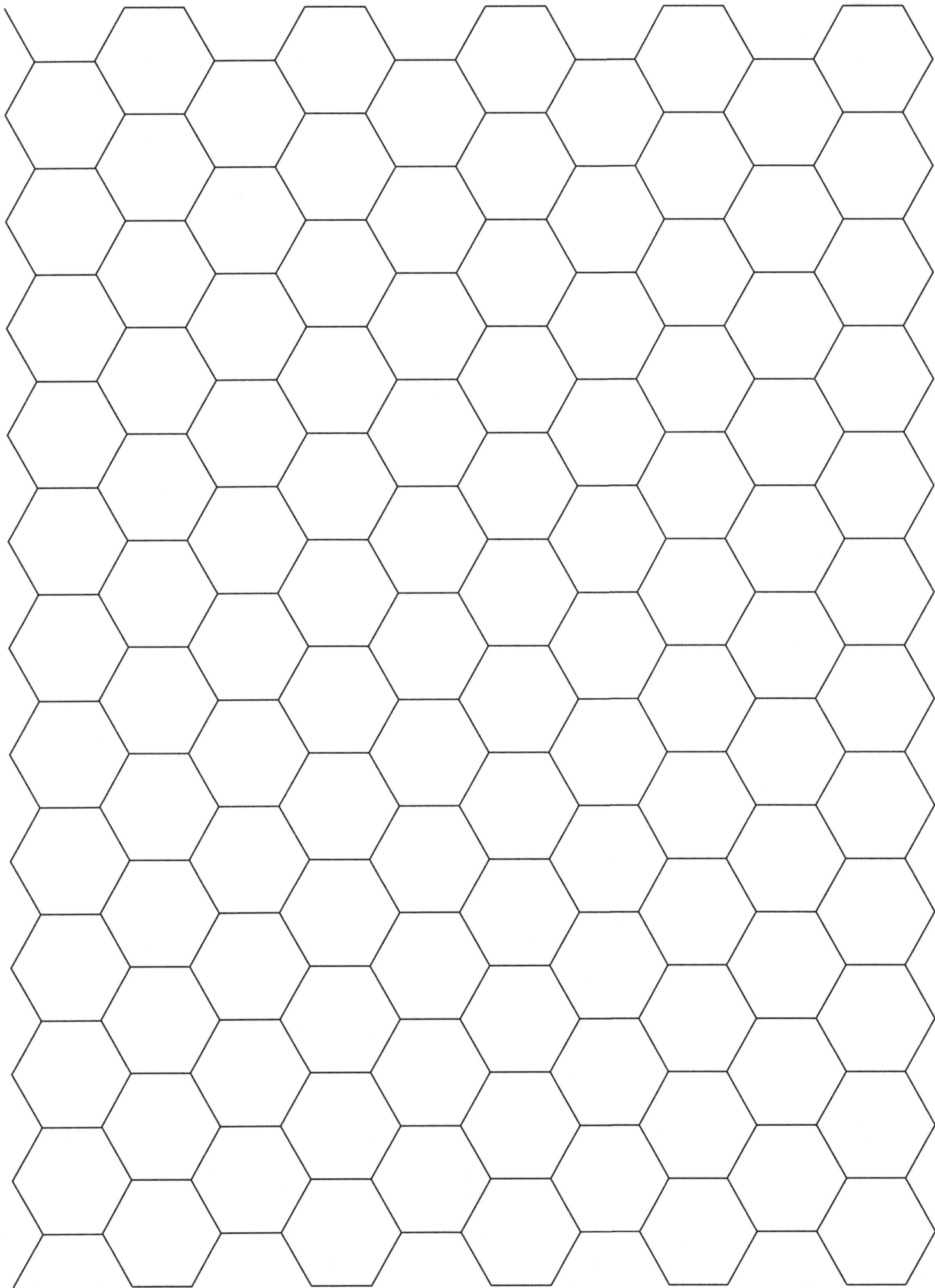

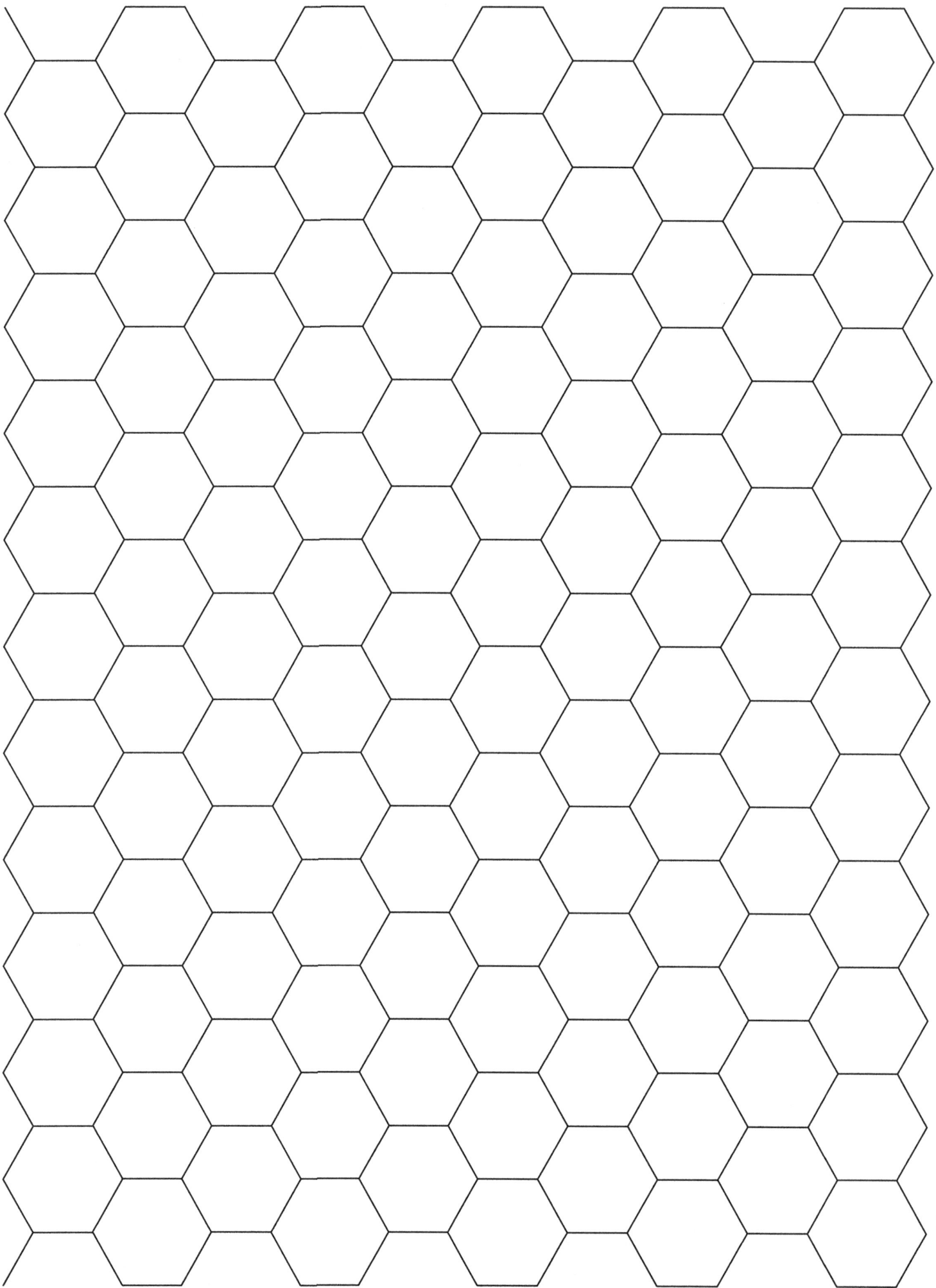

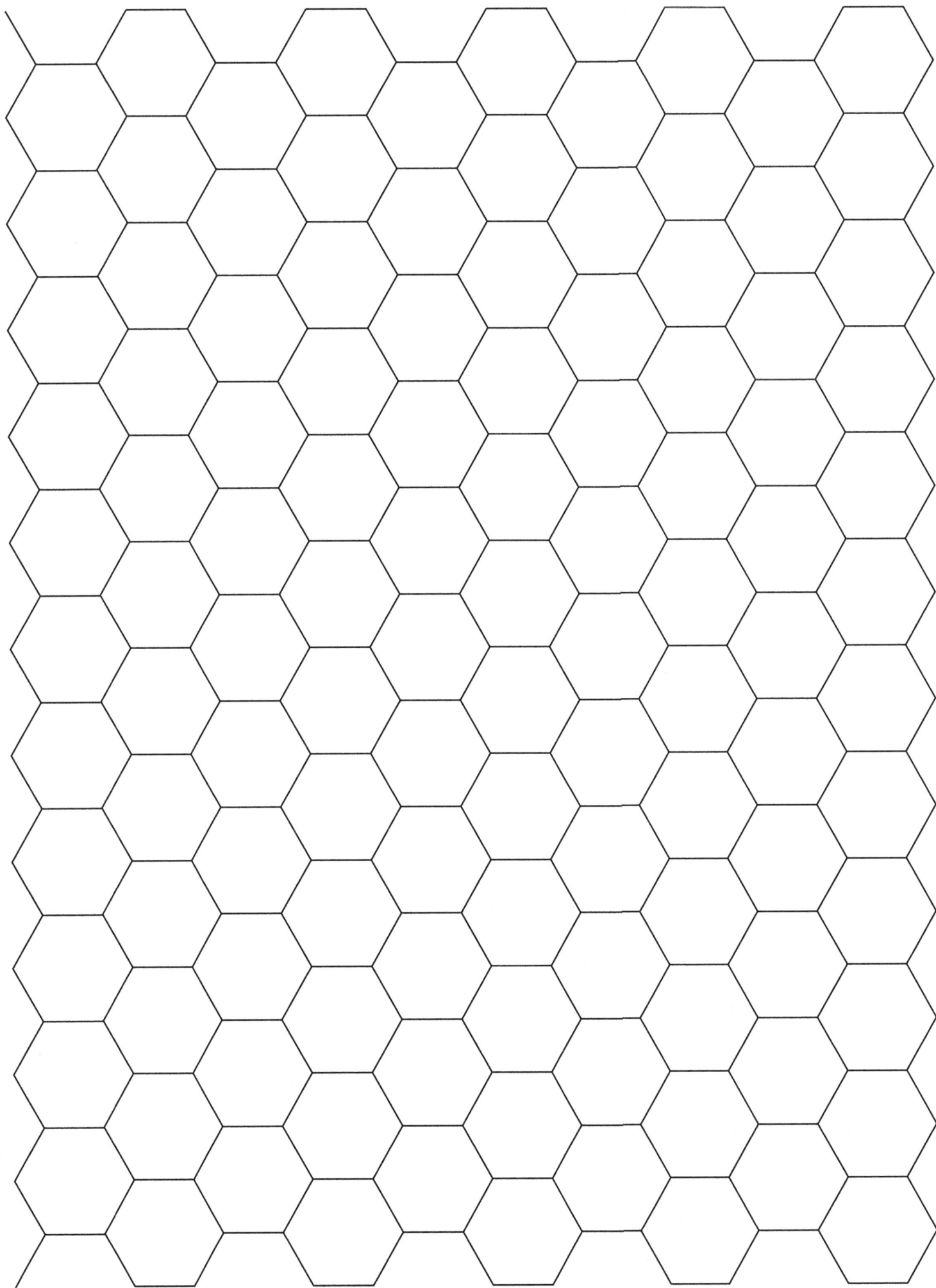

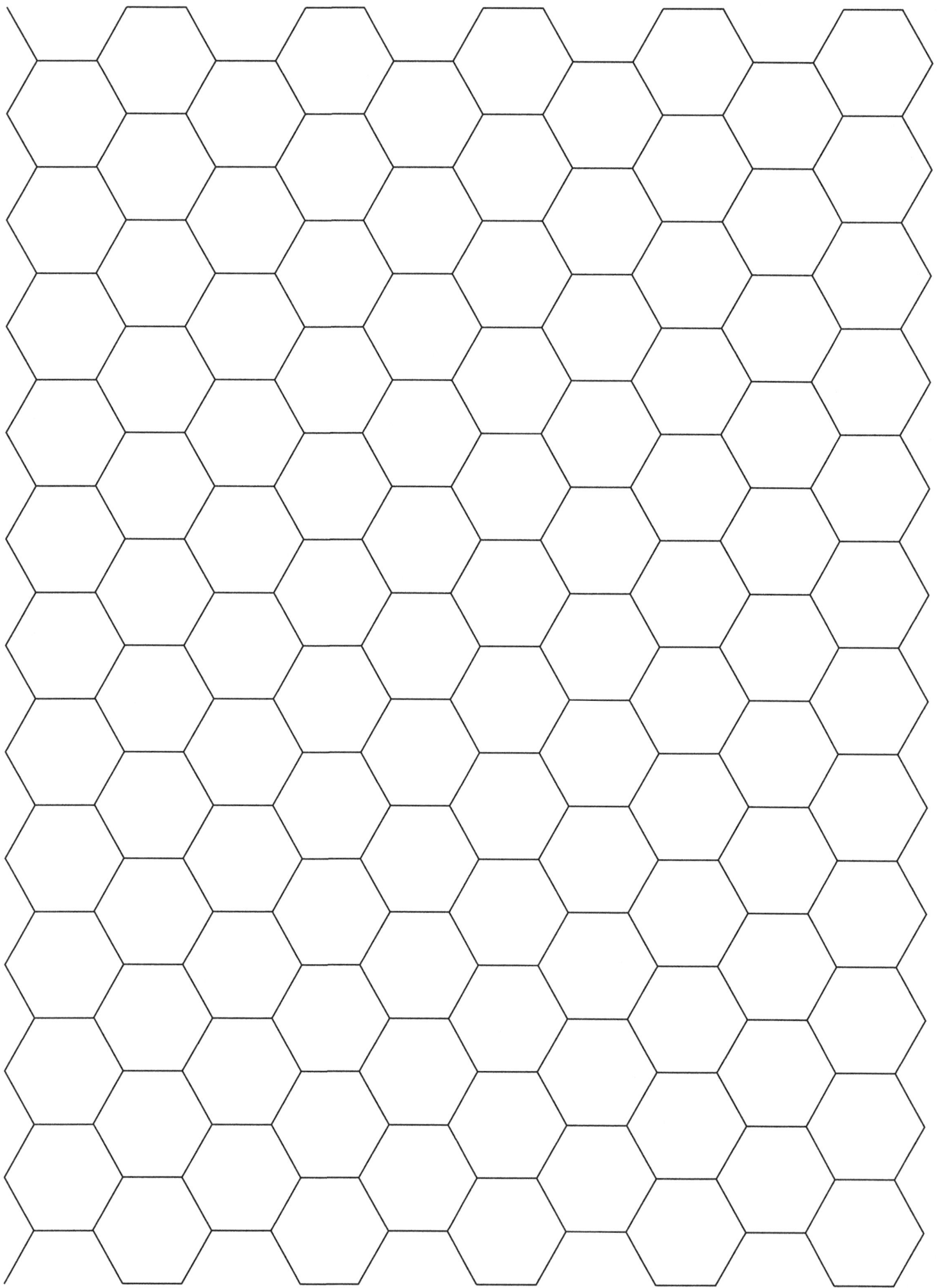

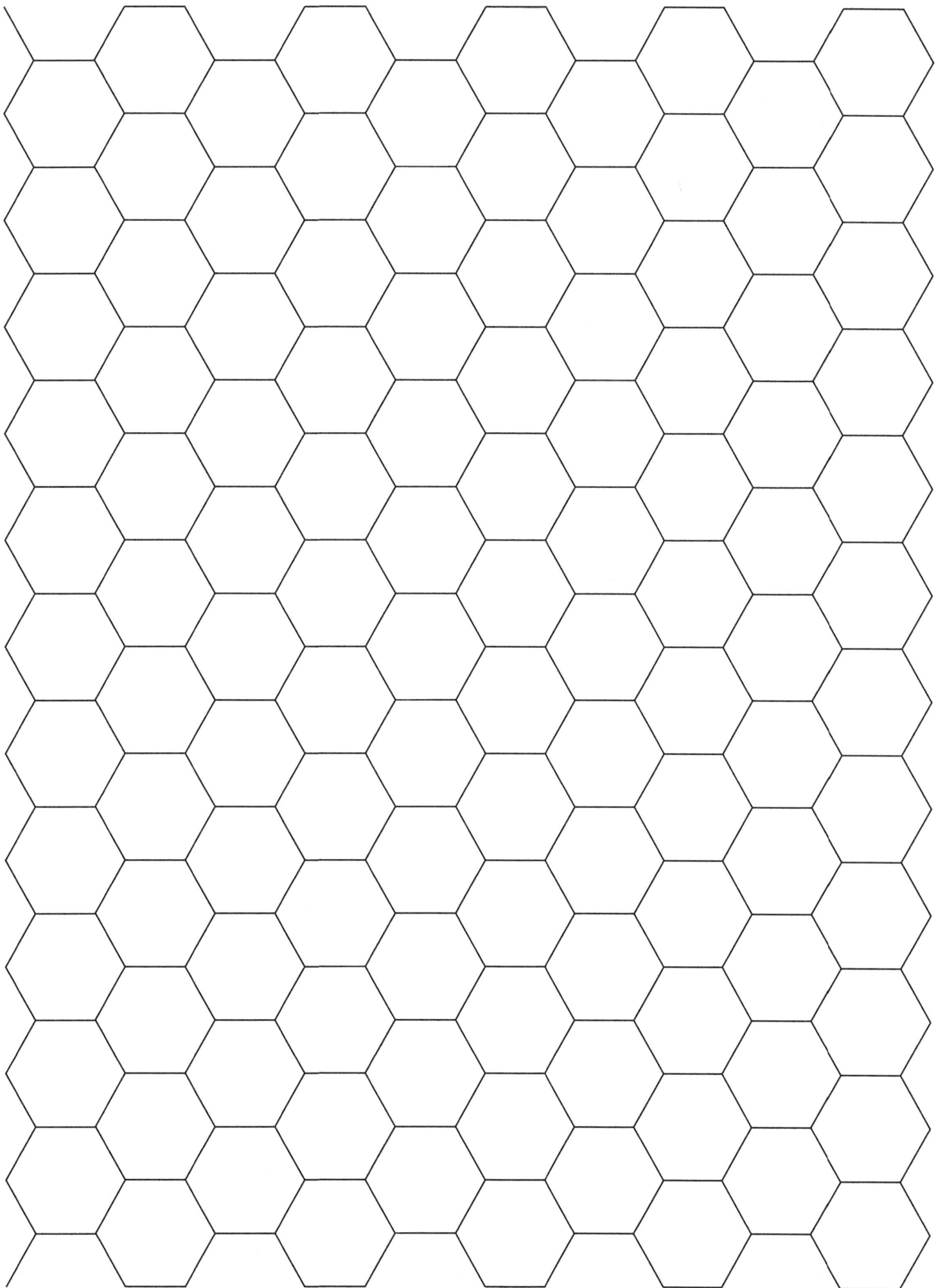

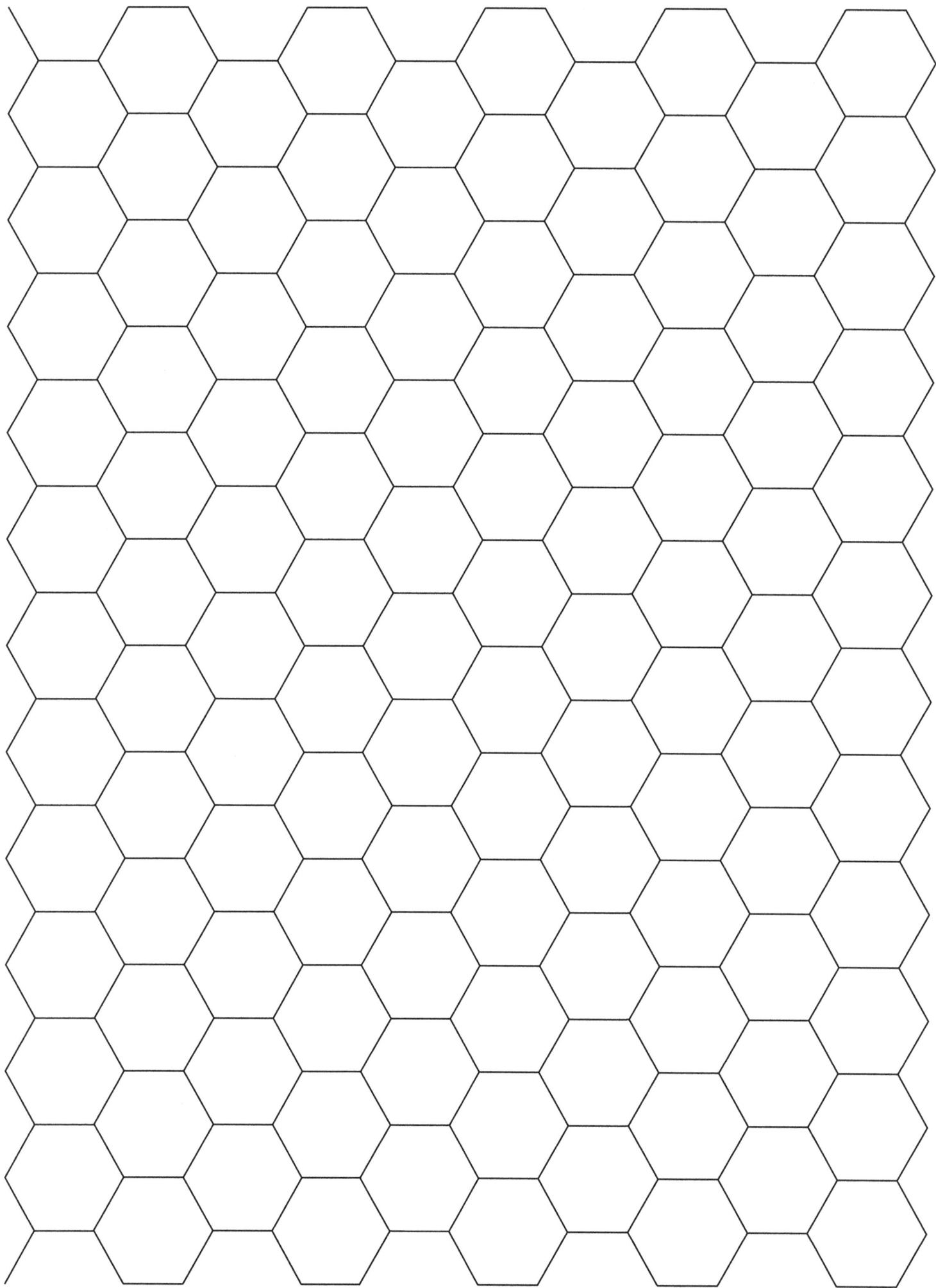

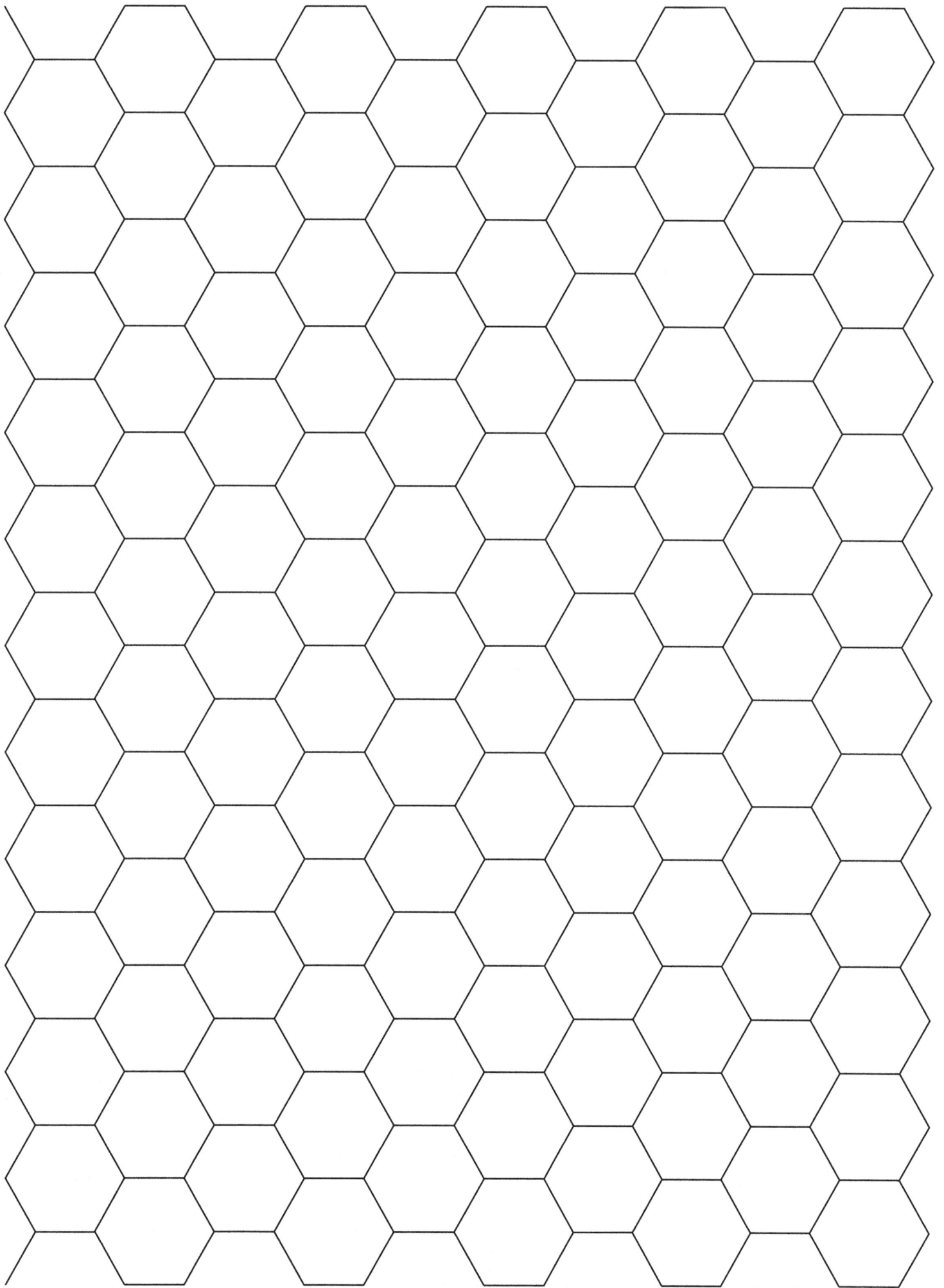

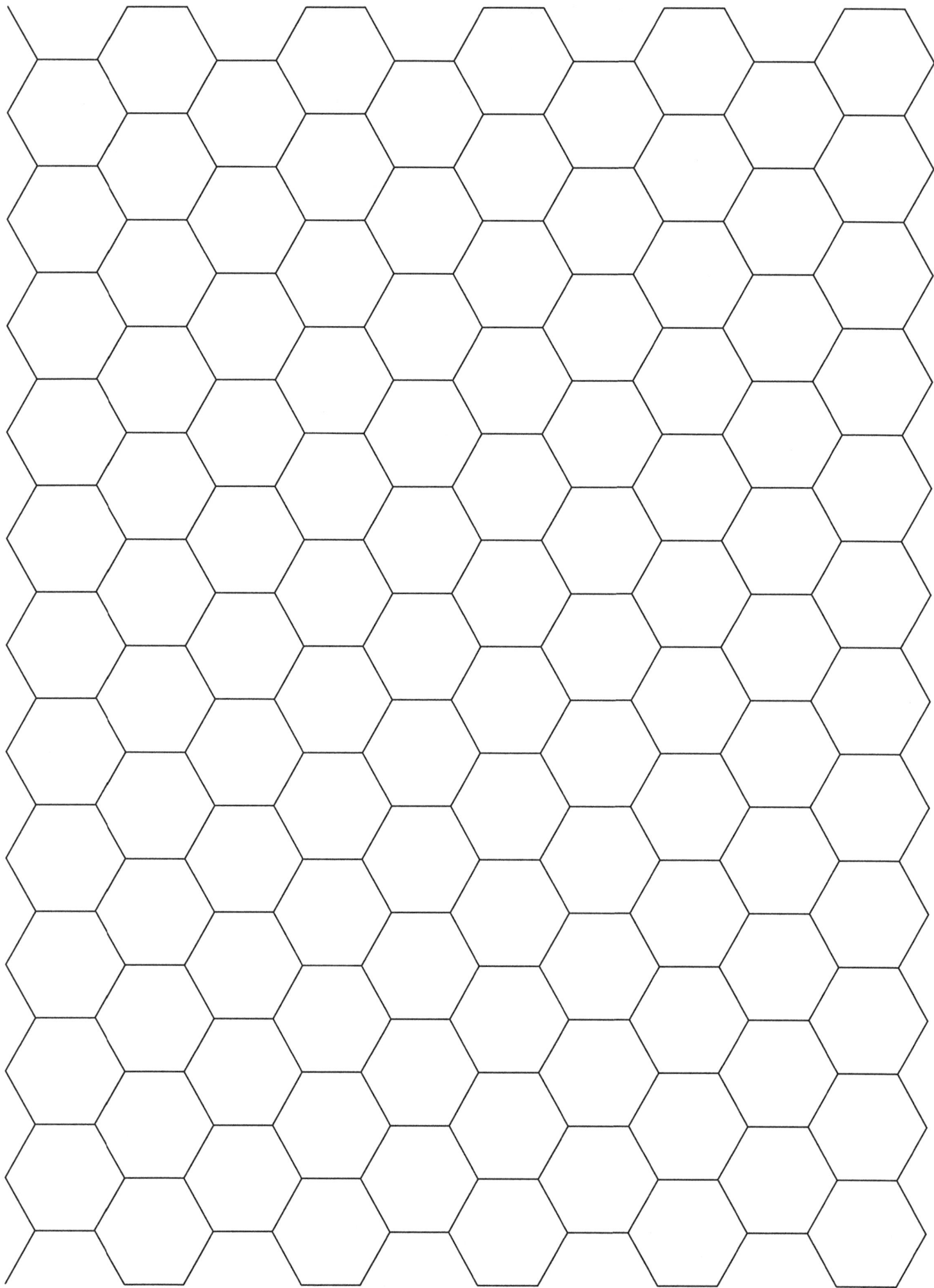

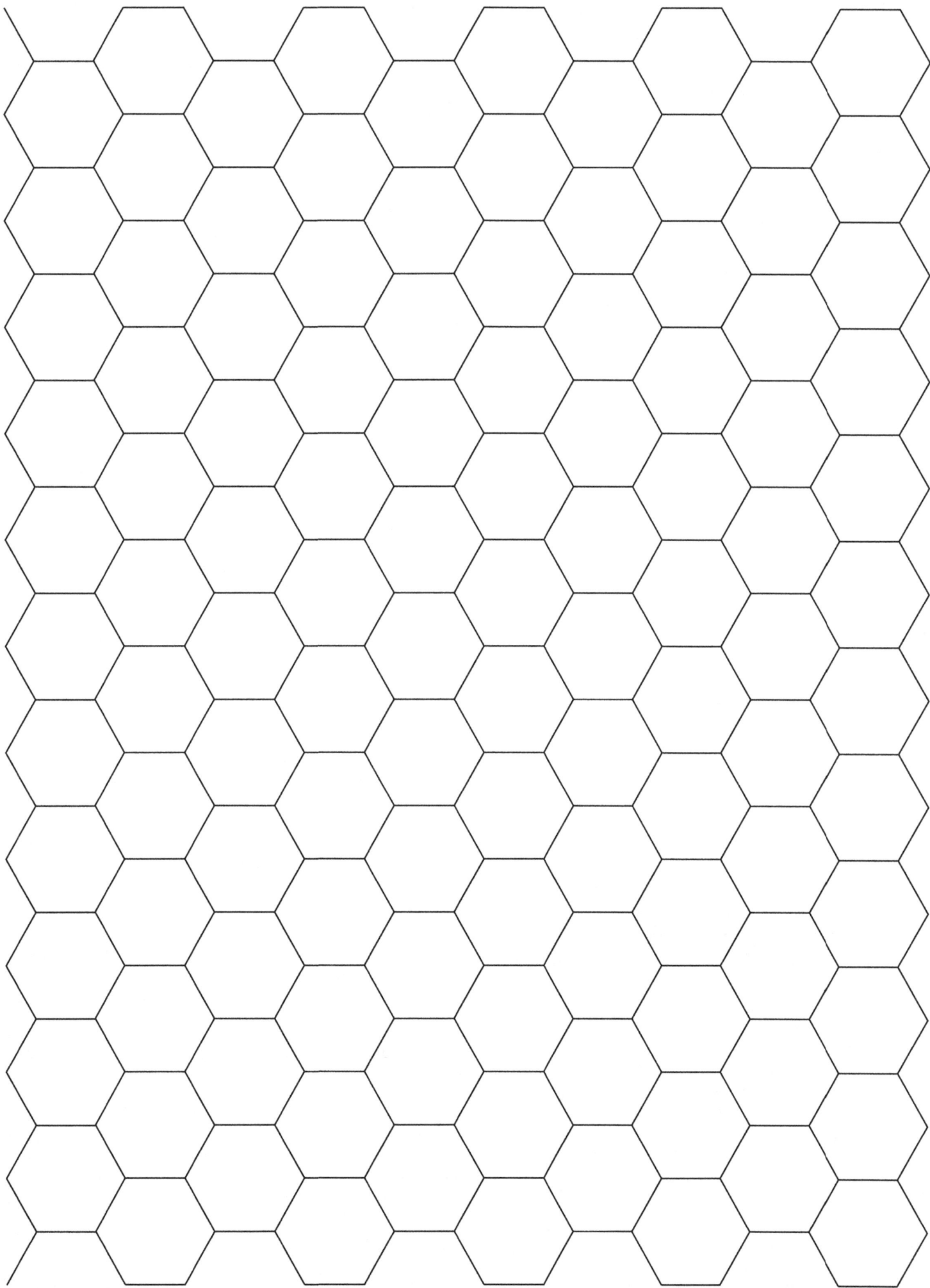

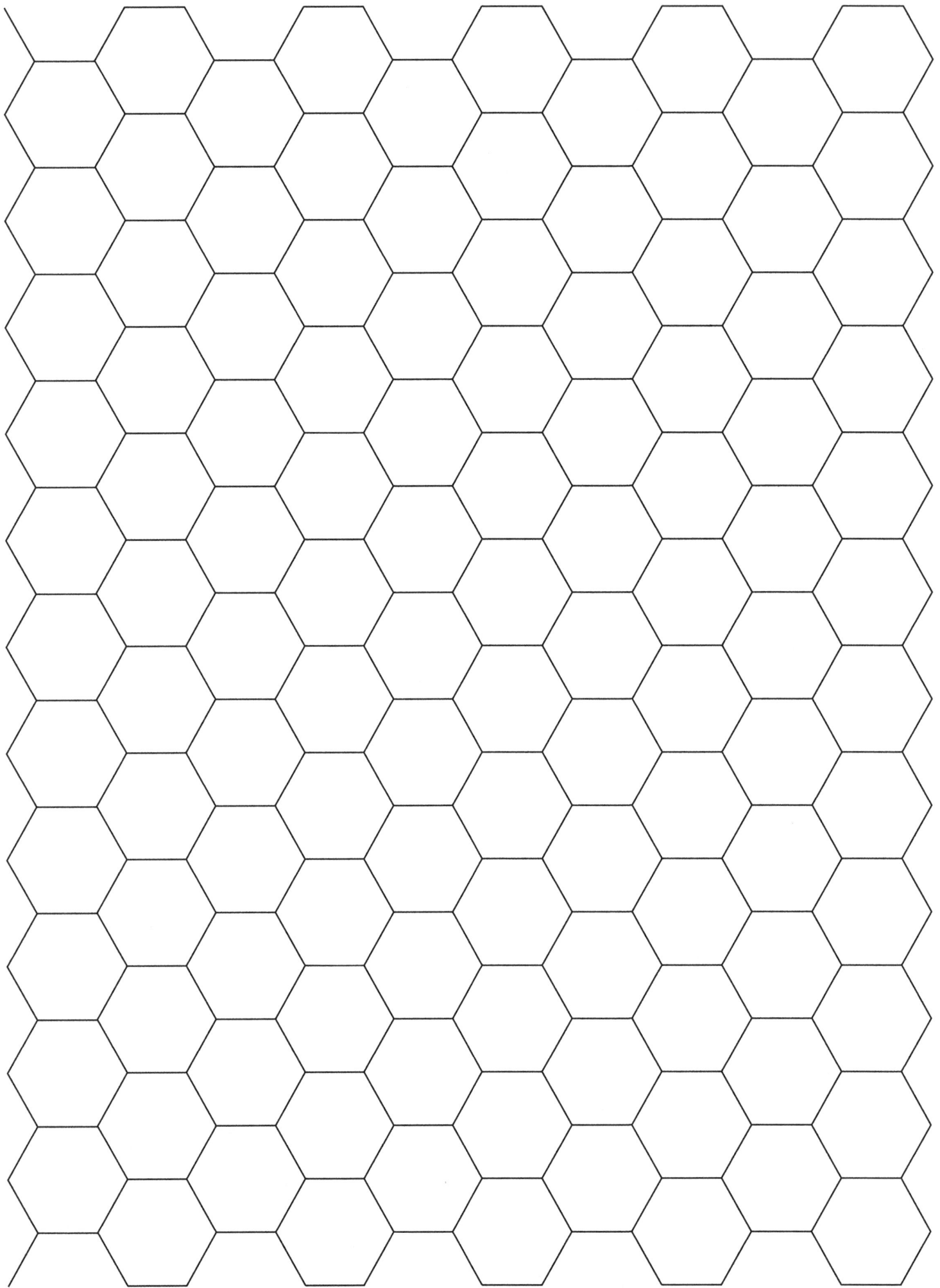

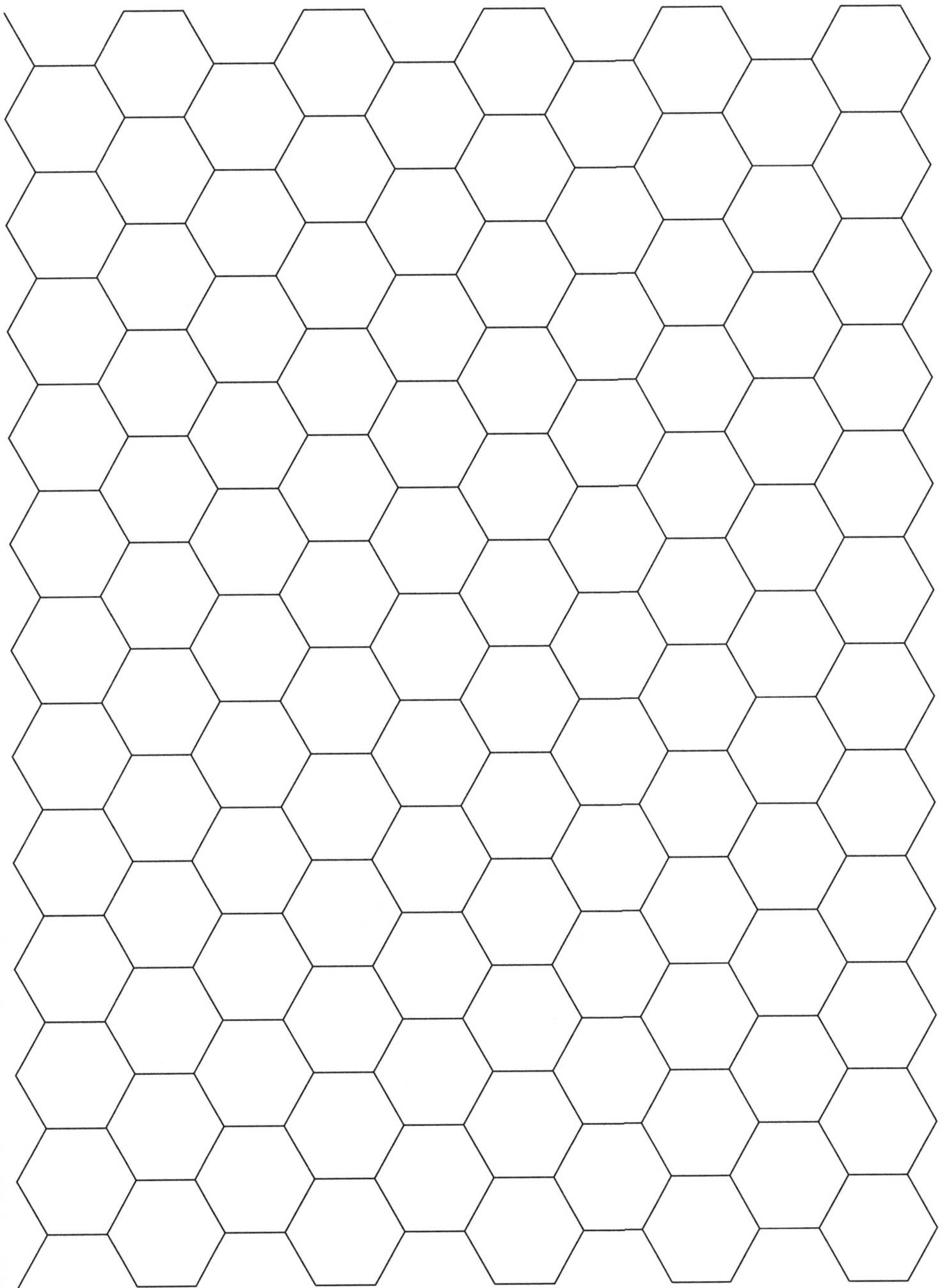

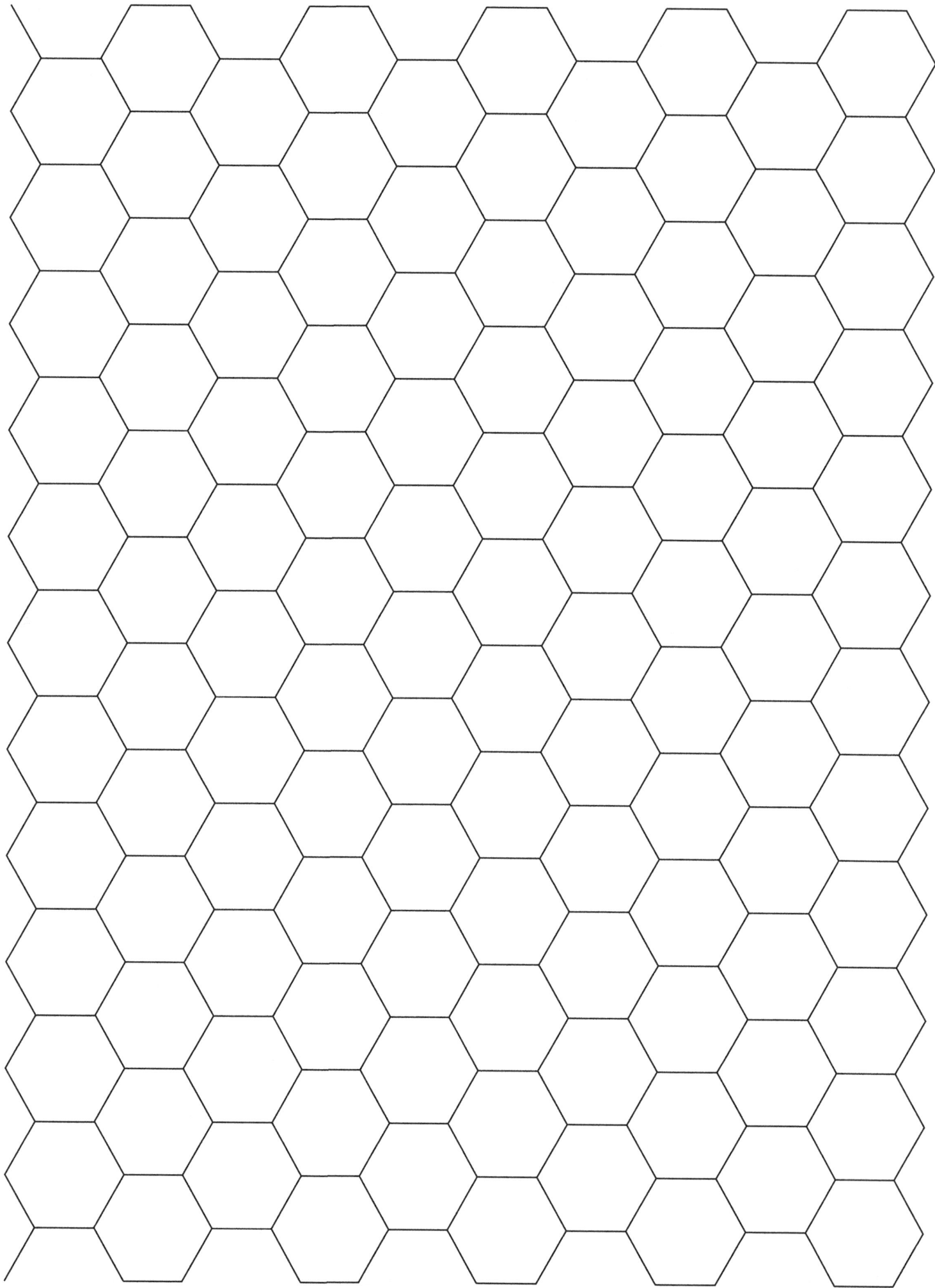

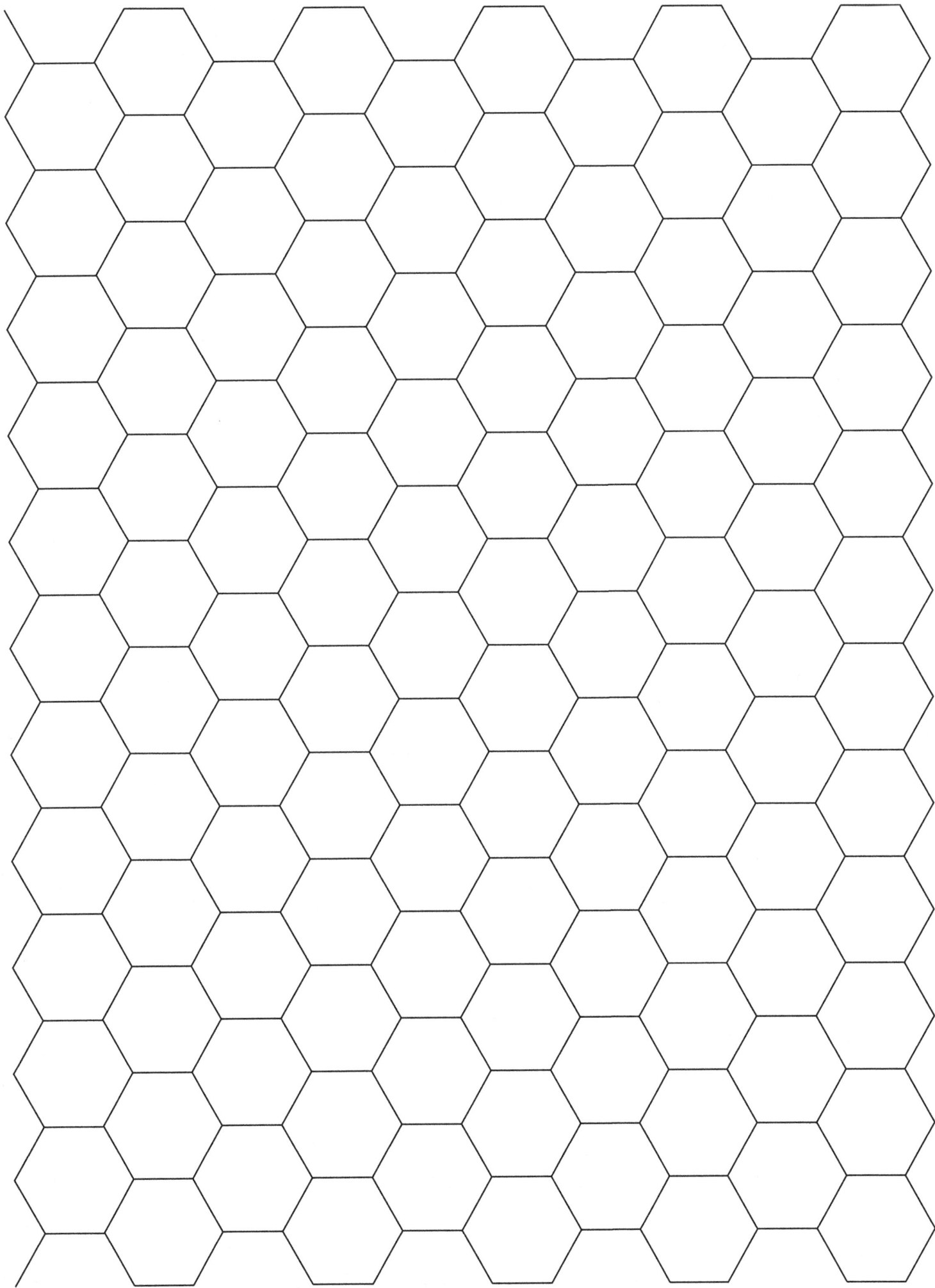

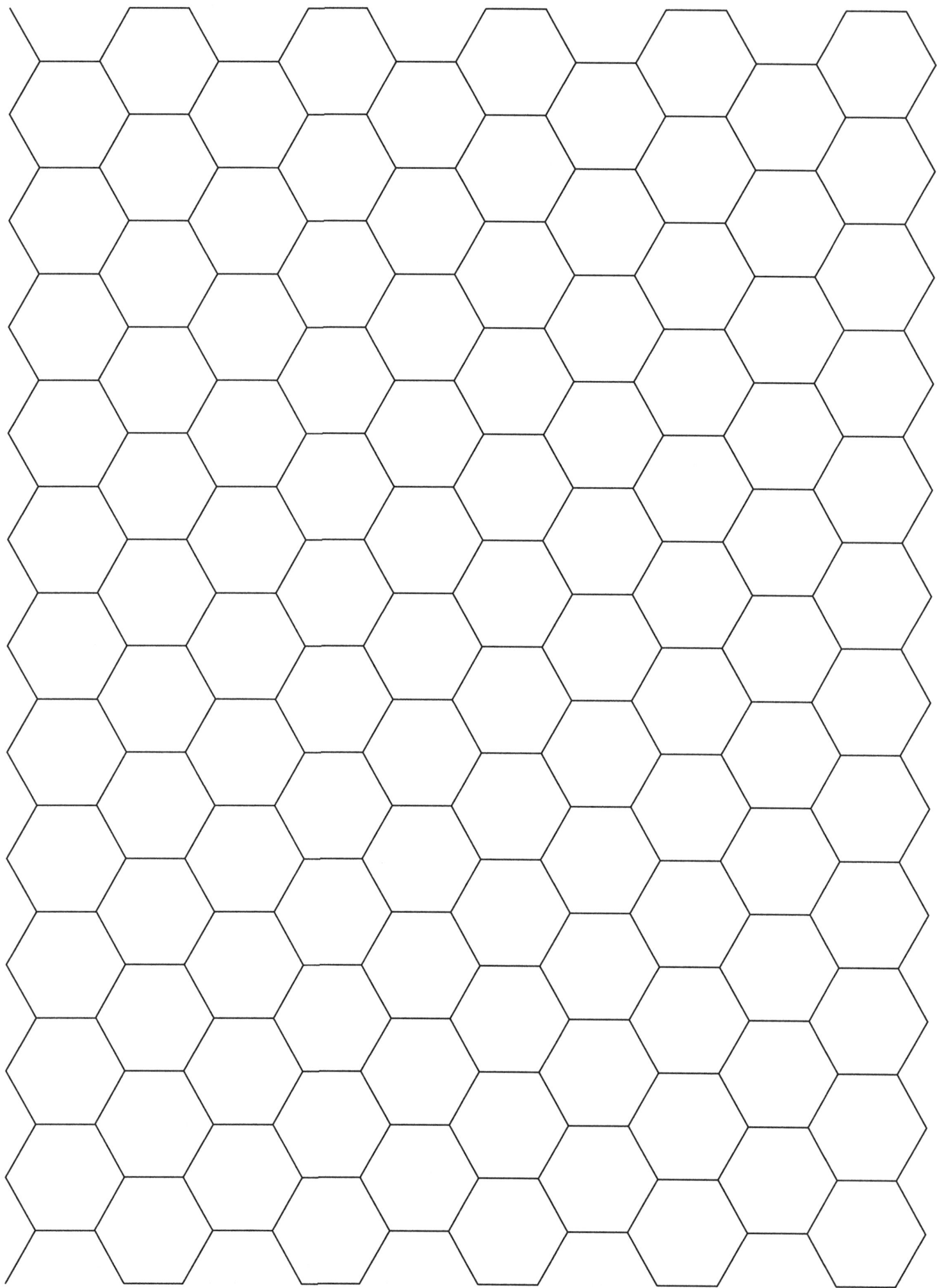

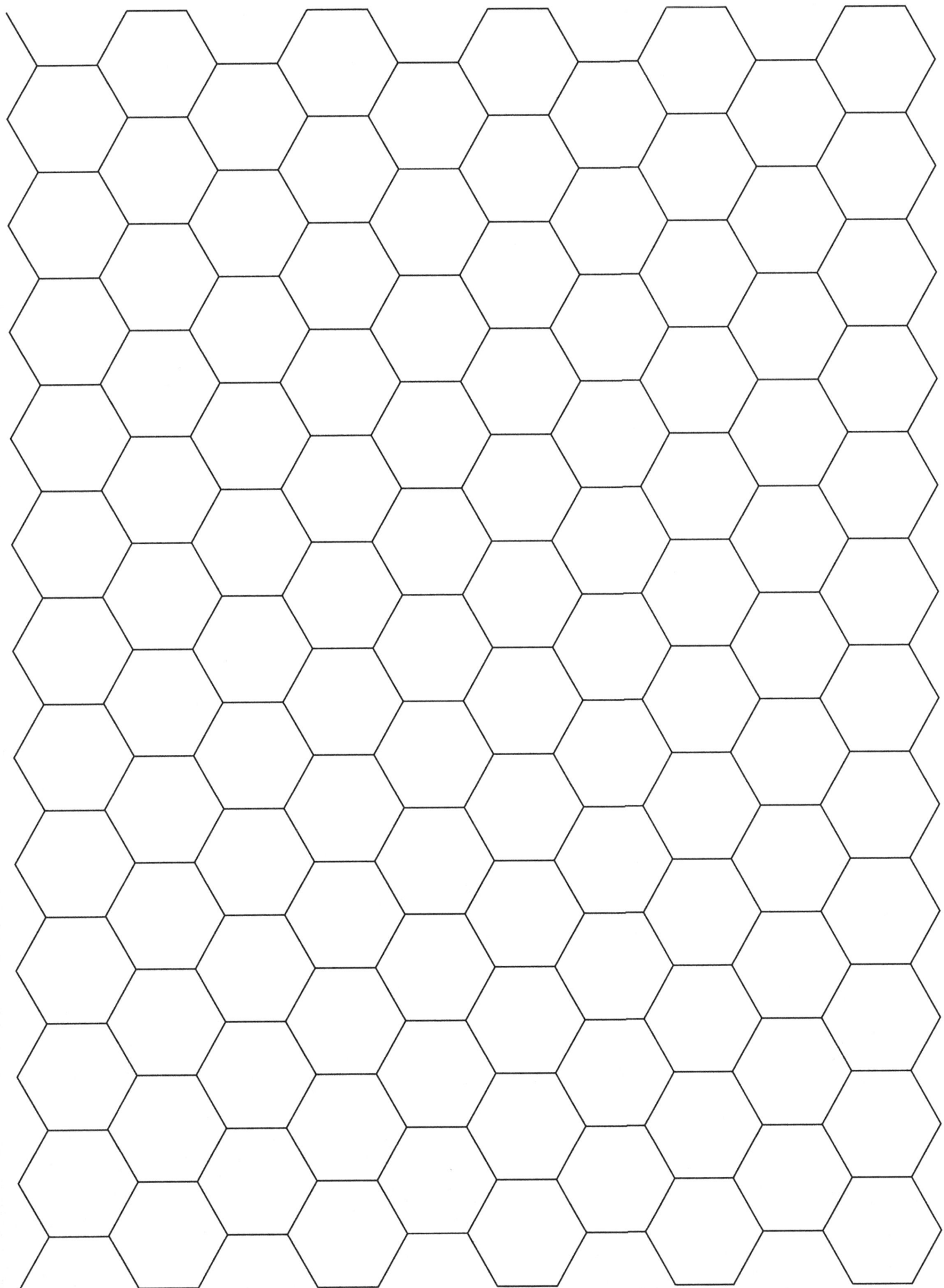

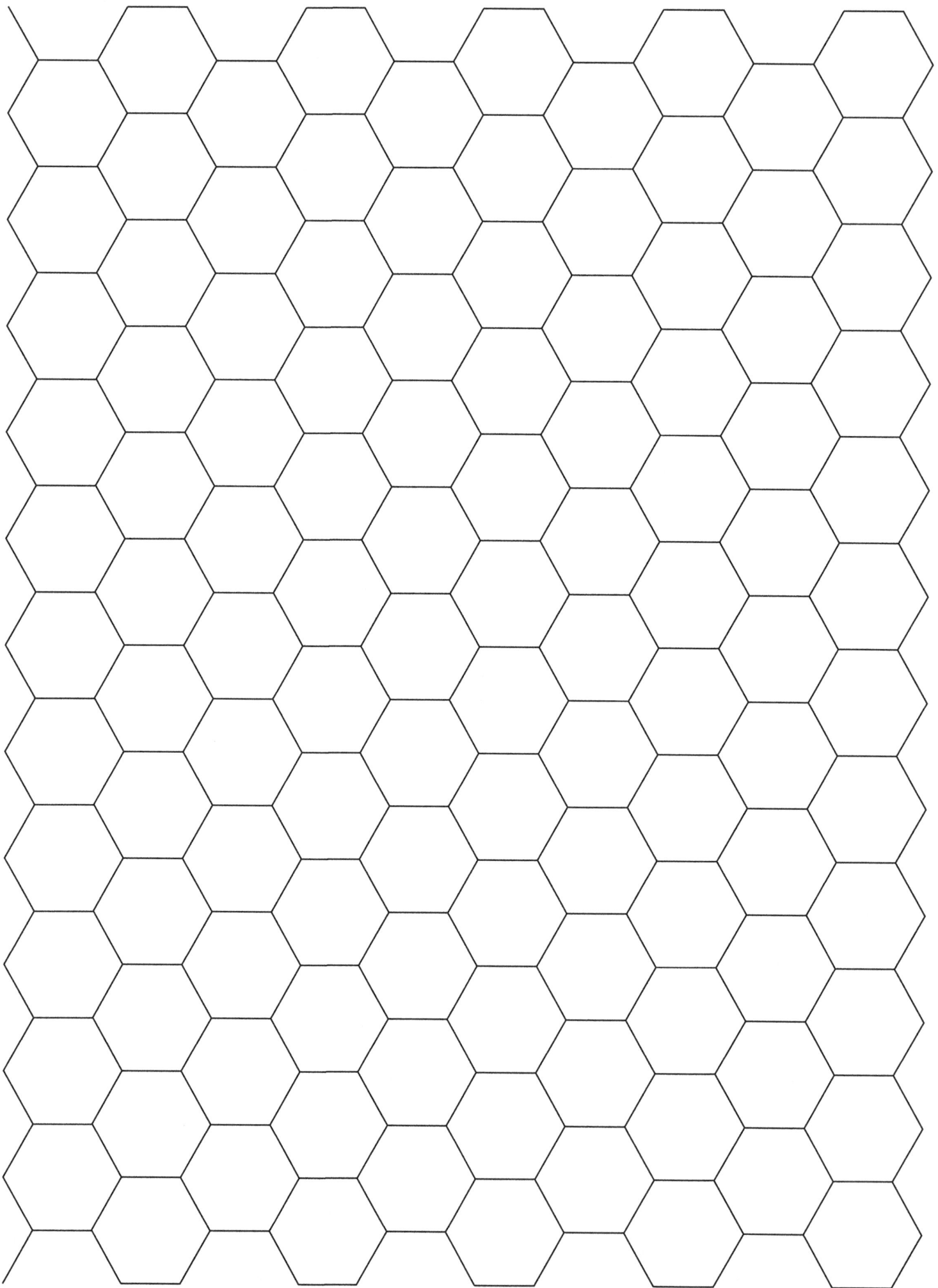

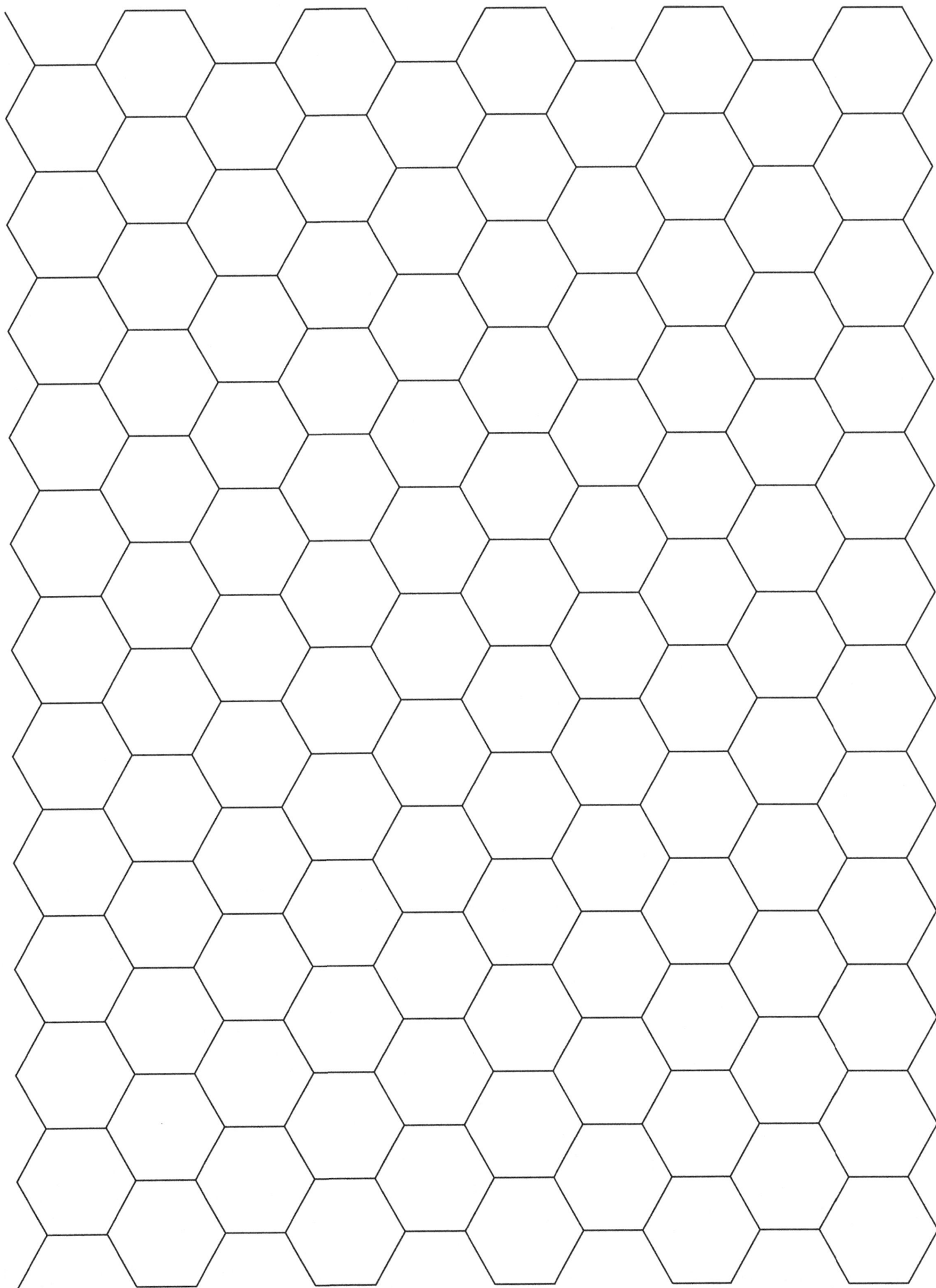

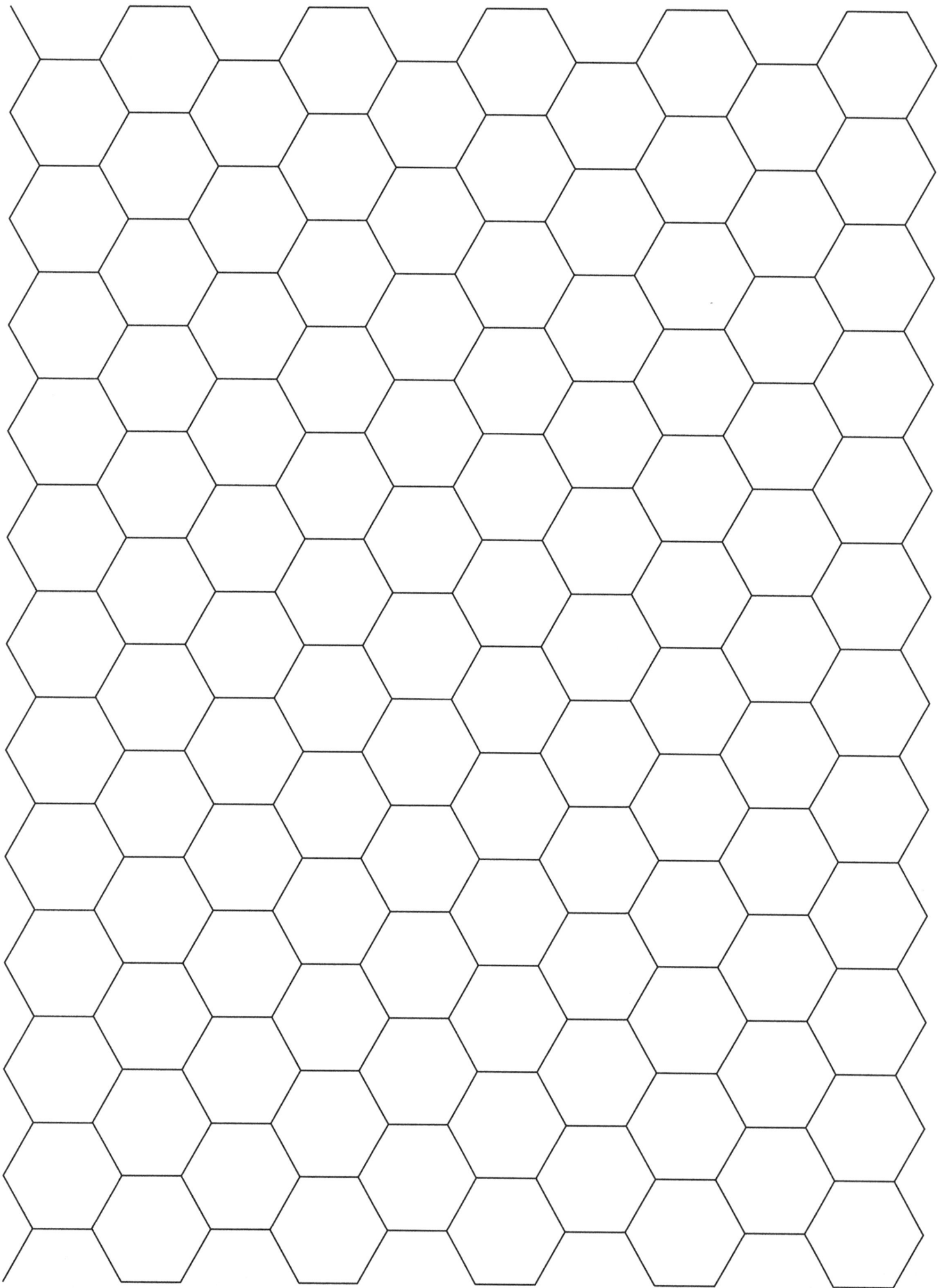

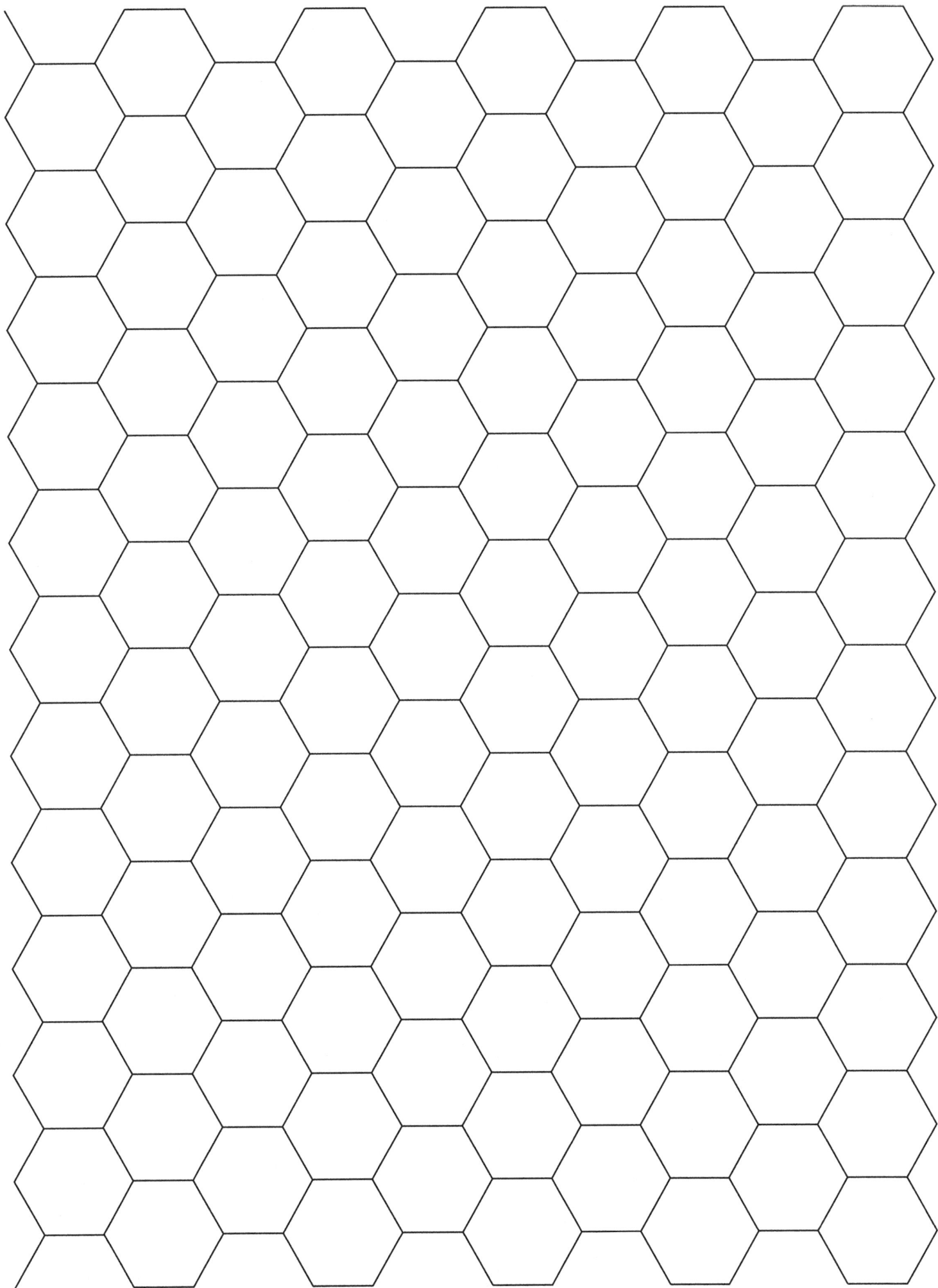

Made in the USA
Middletown, DE
14 March 2021